BEST OF
Aleene's Creative Living
Book 2

Oxmoor House®

Best of Aleene's Creative Living, Book 2
©1998 by Oxmoor House, Inc.
Book Division of Southern Progress Corporation
P.O. Box 2463, Birmingham, Alabama 35201

Published by Oxmoor House, Inc., and Leisure Arts, Inc.

Library of Congress Catalog Card Number: 97-65762
Hardcover ISBN: 0-8487-1675-2
Softcover ISBN: 0-8487-1676-0
Manufactured in the United States of America
First Printing 1998

Editor-in-Chief: Nancy Fitzpatrick Wyatt
Senior Crafts Editor: Susan Ramey Cleveland
Senior Editor, Editorial Services: Olivia Kindig Wells
Art Director: James Boone

Best of Aleene's Creative Living, Book 2
Editor: Lois Martin
Editorial Assistant: Heather Averett
Copy Editor: L. Amanda Owens
Designer: Carol Damsky
Illustrator: Kelly Davis
Director, Production and Distribution: Phillip Lee
Associate Production Manager: Theresa L. Beste
Production Assistant: Faye Porter Bonner

Aleene's Creative Living
Founder: Aleene Jackson
Editor: Tiffany M. Windsor
Managing Editor: Cathy J. Burlingham
Assistant Editor: Joan Fee
Director of Photography: Craig Cook
Senior Photographer: Medeighnia Lentz
Designer/Stylist: Carolyn Bainbridge
Cover Portrait Photographer: Christine Photography

Aleene's™ is a registered trademark of Artis, Inc.
Trademark Registration #1504878
Aleene's™ is used by permission of Artis, Inc.

To order Aleene's products by mail, call Aleene's in California
at 1-800-825-3363.

Projects pictured on cover (clockwise from top left): Whirligig (page 64), Sheer Secrets (page 52), Floral Ornaments (page 126), and Tropical Temptations (page 82).

We're Here for You!
We at Oxmoor House are dedicated to serving you with reliable information that expands your imagination and enriches your life. We welcome your comments and suggestions. Please write us at:
    Oxmoor House, Inc.
    Editor, *Best of Aleene's Creative Living, Book 2*
    2100 Lakeshore Drive
    Birmingham, AL 35209
To order additional publications, call
1-205-877-6560.

Contents

Aleene

Tiffany

Introduction

Since 1992 we've been producing *Aleene's Creative Living* magazine. From a weekly minimagazine with a couple of craft projects per issue, the publication has grown into a 68-page monthly that includes about 40 craft ideas.

Each month, my staff and I review the more than 200 craft projects presented during a month of television shows. We select ones for publication that offer a variety of craft types, skill levels, and uses. Thanks to the support of national crafts stores and major manufacturers, plus the work of top independent designers, we're able to present our readers with fresh, new crafts, featuring innovative products and brand-new techniques.

In 1997 we teamed with Oxmoor House to present a collection of outstanding crafts for home decor, wearables, gifts, and holiday decorations called *Best of Aleene's Creative Living*. Now, we gladly offer even more superb projects in *Best of Aleene's Creative Living, Book 2*. We hope you enjoy making these projects.

Wishing you endless creativity,

Crafting Hints

Tips for Successful Gluing

Aleene and Tiffany give you the benefit of their years of crafting experience with the following suggestions for working with glue.

• To make Aleene's Tacky Glue™ and Aleene's Designer Tacky Glue™ even tackier, leave the lid off for about an hour before use so that excess moisture evaporates.

• Too much glue makes items slip around; it does not provide a better bond. To apply a film of glue to a project, use a cardboard squeegee (see photo below). Cut a 3" square of cardboard (cereal box cardboard works well) and use this squeegee to smooth the glue onto the craft material. Wait a few minutes to let the glue begin to form a skin before putting the items together.

• To squeeze fine lines of glue from a glue bottle, apply a temporary tape tip to the bottle nozzle. Using a 4"-long piece of transparent tape, align 1 long edge of the tape with the edge of the nozzle. Press the tape firmly to the nozzle to prevent leaks. Rotate the glue bottle to wrap the tape around the nozzle. The tape will reverse direction and wind back down toward the bottle. Press the tail of the tape to the bottle for easy removal.

Working with Aleene's Fusible Web

Wash and dry fabrics and garments to remove any sizing before applying fusible web. Do not use fabric softener in the washer or the dryer. Lay the fabric wrong side up on the ironing surface. A hard surface, such as a wooden cutting board, will ensure a firm bond. Lay the fusible web, paper side up, on the fabric (the glue side feels rough). With a hot, dry iron, fuse the web to the fabric by placing and lifting the iron. Do not allow the iron to rest on the web for more than 2 or 3 seconds. Do not slide the iron back and forth across the web.

Transfer the pattern to the paper side of the web and cut out the pattern as specified in the project directions. To fuse the cutout to the project, carefully peel the paper backing from the cutout, making sure the web is attached to the fabric. If the web is still attached to the paper, fuse it again to the fabric cutout before fusing it to the project. Arrange the cutout on the project surface. With a hot, dry iron, fuse the cutout to the project by placing and lifting the iron. Hold the iron on each area of the cutout for approximately 60 seconds.

Metric Conversion Chart

U.S.	Metric
⅛"	3 mm
¼"	6 mm
⅜"	9 mm
½"	1.3 cm
⅝"	1.6 cm
¾"	1.9 cm
⅞"	2.2 cm
1"	2.5 cm
2"	5.1 cm
3"	7.6 cm
4"	10.2 cm
5"	12.7 cm
6"	15.2 cm
7"	17.8 cm
8"	20.3 cm
9"	22.9 cm
10"	25.4 cm
11"	27.9 cm
12"	30.5 cm
36"	91.5 cm
45"	114.3 cm
60"	152.4 cm
⅛ yard	0.11 m
¼ yard	0.23 m
⅓ yard	0.3 m
⅜ yard	0.34 m
½ yard	0.46 m
⅝ yard	0.57 m
⅔ yard	0.61 m
¾ yard	0.69 m
⅞ yard	0.8 m
1 yard	0.91 m

To Convert to Metric Measurements:

When you know:	Multiply by:	To find:
inches (")	25	millimeters (mm)
inches (")	2.5	centimeters (cm)
inches (")	0.025	meters (m)
feet (')	30	centimeters (cm)
feet (')	0.3	meters (m)
yards	90	centimeters (cm)
yards	0.9	meters (m)

Decorative

In the following pages, you'll find fantastic ideas for all sorts of fast and fun projects to decorate your home.

Page 19

Page 14

Accents

SATIN SHEEN CHAIRS

Materials

For each: Plastic chair
Chair pad
For yellow-white-and-red chair:
Aleene's Satin Sheen Twisted
Ribbon™: 5 yards each
yellow, white, red (See note.)
For watermelon chair: Aleene's
Satin Sheen Twisted Ribbon™:
5 yards red, 2½ yards green,
2 yards white (See note.)
Felt-tip permanent black marker

Directions

Note: Yardages may vary.
Choose colors of Satin Sheen to
match chair pad. Satin Sheen is
waterproof and won't fade.

1 **For yellow-white-and-red
chair,** untwist all yardages
of twisted ribbon. Cut each
length in half widthwise. Cut red
ribbon in half lengthwise.

2 Weave ribbons in and out of
rungs, starting at bottom and
using yellow. Weave in following
order to fill: yellow, white, red,
white, and yellow. Leave 5" tail at
beginning and end of each ribbon
length and tuck tails in back. Wrap
top edge with red (see photo).

3 **For watermelon chair,**
untwist all yardages of twisted
ribbon. Weave ribbons in and out
of rungs, starting at bottom and
using green, white, and red to fill
(see photo). Leave 5" tail at
beginning and end of each ribbon
length and tuck tails in back.
Draw seeds with marker.

4 **For each,** tie purchased
pad onto chair.

Perk up inexpensive patio chairs with these easy-to-do makeovers.

Designs by Cheryl Ball, SCD

Seed

Watermelon Plate

Turn a clear plate into a slice of summer.

Materials
Glass plate with scalloped edge
Pop-up craft sponge
**Aleene's Premium-Coat™ Acrylic
    Paints: True Green, Deep
    Green, Black, Medium Pink,
    True Red**
**Aleene's Enhancers™: Glazing
    Medium**
Waxed paper
Wooden craft sticks
Paper towels
Thick kitchen sponge

Directions

1 Wash and dry plate. Cut pop-up sponge to match 1 scallop on plate rim. Place sponge in water to expand and wring out excess water.

2 Pour small puddle of each color of paint onto waxed paper. For each, mix equal parts paint and Glazing Medium, using craft stick. Dip sponge into True Green and blot excess on paper towel. Press sponge onto every other scallop on plate rim, working from back of plate (see photo). Let dry. Sponge-paint with second coat of True Green. Repeat to sponge-paint 2 coats of Deep Green onto remaining scallops on plate rim.

3 Transfer seed pattern to remaining pop-up sponge and cut out. Place sponge in water to expand and wring out excess water. Sponge-paint seeds at center of plate, using Black (see photo). Let dry. Sponge-paint with second coat. Let dry.

4 Use kitchen sponge to paint circle in center of plate with Medium Pink (see photo). Let dry. Sponge-paint with second coat. Let dry.

5 Sponge-paint to edge of center section with True Red, covering seeds. Let dry. Sponge-paint with second coat. Let dry.

6 Let paint dry for 72 hours before using. To clean, wipe with damp sponge.

Summer Breeze

Bring the beach home with the shells and the waves of this lamp and matching wreath.

Lamp

Materials
Wooden lamp with shade
Aleene's Premium-Coat™ Acrylic Paints: Blush, Dusty Blush, Dusty Sage, Soft Sage, Ivory, Light Yellow
Paintbrushes: #6 flat, 10/0 liner
Fine sandpaper
Tack cloth
Aleene's Thick Designer Tacky Glue™
Small shells
Silk greens

Directions

1 Paint lamp base Blush. Let dry. Paint top and bottom of base Dusty Blush. Let dry. Lightly sand lamp to give weathered look. Wipe lamp with tack cloth to remove any dust. If desired, paint with second coat. Let dry.

2 Use flat paintbrush to paint thick wavy lines (see photo and Diagram on page 12); paint some lines Dusty Sage and some Soft Sage. For other lines, mix both colors on brush to add dimension. Let dry.

3 Use liner brush to paint thin wavy lines in Dusty Sage, Soft Sage, or combination (see photo).

Lamp Design by Barbara Baruti for A.C. Moore
Wreath Design by Joan Fee, SCD

Use tip of brush to add dots of Blush, Dusty Blush, Ivory, and Light Yellow. (Do not wash brush after each use.) Let dry.

4 Referring to Diagram on page 12, paint shade to match base. Let dry. Glue shells to base as desired. Let dry. Cut small pieces from silk greens and glue between shells. Let dry.

Wreath

Materials
Aleene's Thick Designer Tacky Glue™
Moss
Straw wreath form
Aleene's Botanical Preserved Flowers & Foliage™: green plumosus, pink and white delphinium, dusty rose gypsophila
Assorted shells
4" length florist's wire

Directions
1 Glue moss to cover front and sides of wreath form. Let dry.

2 Cut plumosus at stems. Glue to cover front and sides of wreath. Let dry.

3 Randomly glue shells to wreath, tucking them into plumosus for wispy look. Let dry.

4 Cut delphinium and gypsophila from stems. Glue randomly around wreath. Let dry.

5 For hanger, make loop from florist's wire and twist ends to secure. Glue to wrong side of wreath at center top. Let dry.

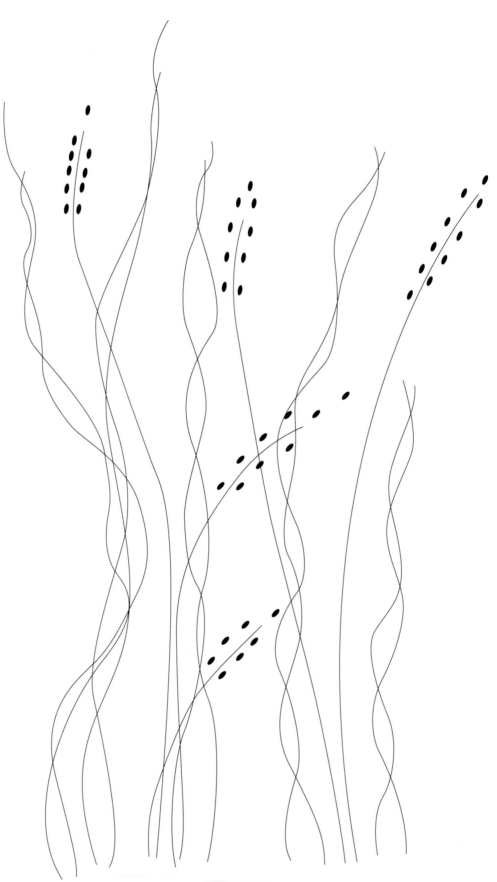

Diagram

Suspended Still Life

Use this technique to silhouette any flat keepsake between glass.

Design by Darsee Lett and Pattie Donham

Materials

For each: Aleene's Reverse Collage Glue™

Disposable or acrylic paintbrush

2 glass panes in desired size

Pressed leaves and flowers

Aleene's 3-D Foiling Glue™

Paper or plastic cups

Aleene's Silver Crafting Foil™

Directions for 1 still life

Hint: Use 4" x 4" glass panes to make a fabulous coaster set.

1 Apply generous amount of Reverse Collage Glue to 1 side of 1 glass pane. Lay flowers and leaves facedown in glue as desired. Apply second coat of glue over leaves and flowers. Let dry.

2 Apply 3-D Foiling Glue to edges of both panes. Place glass panes on upside-down cups so that edges do not touch anything. Let dry overnight.

3 To apply silver foil to each edge of glass pane, lay foil dull side down on top of glue line. Using finger, gently but firmly press foil onto glue, completely covering glue with foil. Peel away foil paper. If any part of glue lines is exposed, reapply foil as needed.

Garden Fence Bookends

As your library grows, keep your volumes in a row with these blooming bookends.

Materials

Aleene's Premium-Coat™ Acrylic Paints: Medium Lavender, Medium Fuchsia, Ivory
Waxed paper
2 (3½"-diameter) clay pots with plates
½" flat shader paintbrush
Cotton swabs
Aleene's Enhancers™: Satin Varnish
Ruler
8 small fence posts (found at lumber warehouse)
Saw (optional)
Aleene's Thick Designer Tacky Glue™
Metal L-shaped bookends
Aleene's Tack-It Over & Over™
Craft or florist's foam
Aleene's Botanical Preserved Flowers and Foliage™: light green boxwood, pink and blue delphinium, yellow statice sinuata, seafoam gypsophila

Directions

1 Paint clay pots Medium Lavender, clay plates Medium Fuchsia, and fence posts Ivory. Let dry. Use cotton swabs to dot Ivory randomly on pots, plates, and posts. Let dry.

2 Apply 1 coat of varnish on all pieces. Let dry. Measure and mark desired height on each post. Trim if necessary. Glue fence posts together with Tacky Glue. Let dry.

3 Lay each bookend flat over edge of table, with long piece pointing up. Apply Tack-It Over & Over to back of long pieces. Let dry overnight.

4 To assemble flowerpots, insert small amount of foam into pots. Cut sprigs of boxwood and arrange in foam (see photo). Add sprigs of delphinium. Fill empty spots with statice and gypsophila.

5 Press fence into Tack-It Over & Over on bookends. Apply Tacky Glue to plate and press pot into glue. Let dry. Apply Tacky Glue to bookend extension and press bottom of plate into glue. Let dry.

Design by Cheryl Ball, SCD

Country Home

Purchased birdhouses and Aleene's Fusible Web™ make these no-sew window treatments a lark to make.

Curtains

Materials

For each: ½ yard fabric
Aleene's Fusible Web™
Ruler
Disappearing-ink pen
½"- to ¾"-diameter dowel (equal in length to window)
Hammer and nails
For birdhouse window: 2 wooden birdhouses with grapevine accents
Drill with appropriate bits
2 sawtooth picture hangers
For hearts window: 2 papier-mâché boxes
Craft knife
Aleene's Enhancers™: All-Purpose Primer
Aleene's Premium-Coat™ Acrylic Paints in desired colors
Assorted paintbrushes

Directions

Note: See page 5 for tips on working with fusible web.

1 Wash and dry fabric; do not use fabric softener in washer or dryer. Iron out any wrinkles.

2 Turn 1 long edge of fabric ½" to wrong side. Fuse ½"-wide strip of fusible web to folded edge. Turn edge under and fuse for hem. Repeat to hem short edges.

3 For rod pocket and top ruffle, fold raw edge of fabric ½" to wrong side. Fuse ½"-wide strip of fusible web to folded edge. Do not remove paper backing. Measure and mark line 6½" from top folded edge on wrong side, using disappearing-ink pen. Position ½"-wide strip of fusible web over line; fuse. Do not remove paper backing. Measure and mark 4"

from top folded edge of fabric. Fold to wrong side; press. Fabric edge with fusible web strip attached should be 4" below new fold and 1½" below second strip of fusible web. Remove paper backing from both strips of fusible web and press for 30 seconds in each section. Place dowel into pocket of curtain.

4 For end pieces, cut 1 hole equal to diameter of dowel in side of each end piece. (Use drill for wood and craft knife for papier-mâché.) For hearts, apply 1 coat of primer to each. Let dry. Paint as desired. Let dry.

5 Insert dowel into holes. For hangers on wood pieces, nail sawtooth picture hanger to back of each end piece. For hangers on papier-mâché, nail bottom of box to wall and then place lid on box.

Designs by Joan Fee, SCD

Braid

Materials
Serrated knife
Florist's foam
3 (2½"-diameter) clay pots
Aleene's Thick Designer Tacky Glue™
Moss
Aleene's Botanical Preserved Flowers and Foliage™: yellow natural yarrow, boxwood, natural lavender, white Australian daisies, rosebuds
Raffia: braid, lengths
Small dried pink flowers

Directions

1 Cut foam to fill pots. Glue 1 piece of foam into each pot. Let dry. Glue moss onto foam to cover. Let dry.

2 Referring to photo, insert dried flowers and foliage into pots, trimming stem lengths as necessary. Cut yarrow very short; use boxwood on outer edges and then fill in with lavender and daisies.

3 Glue pots to braid (see photo). Let dry. Divide pink dried flowers into thirds. Holding several lengths together, tie raffia in bow around 1 bunch of flowers. Repeat with remaining bunches. Then glue 1 bunch of flowers under each pot. Let dry. Cut rosebuds and leaves and glue to each bunch of flowers at bow. Let dry.

Design by Jan Blackwell

Birdhouse Buffet

If you can blow through an ordinary drinking straw, you can create this fun finish for a birdhouse.

Materials
Birdfeeder
Sandpaper
Tack cloth
Aleene's Enhancers™: All-Purpose Primer, Gloss Varnish
Sponge brush
Aleene's Premium-Coat™ Acrylic Paints: White, desired colors from light palette
Plastic drinking straw

Directions

Note: Use birdfeeder outdoors in protected area or place in large indoor potted plant. If using indoors, add Spanish moss and wooden eggs speckled in coordinating colors.

1 Sand birdfeeder smooth. Wipe birdfeeder with tack cloth to remove any dust. Apply 1 coat of primer. Let dry. Sand again to smooth out wood grain; wipe clean.

2 Apply 1 coat of White or desired color. Dilute each color of desired decorative paint with equal parts water. Mix well. Place small amount of 1 diluted color on feeder. (You can keep birdfeeder level or tilt it to help direct paint.) Blow air through straw to force paint puddle to spread out. Let dry. Repeat with all colors until desired pattern is achieved. Apply 1 coat of varnish to birdfeeder. Let dry.

Starflower Quilt Afghan

A festival of crocheted flowers in bright colors brings a little bit of spring to any setting.

Materials

**3.5-ounce skeins Caron Wintuck®
worsted-weight yarn: 4 skeins
each Spring Meadow (A) and
Dark Sage (B); 1 skein each
Light Yellow (C), Apricot (D),
Persimmon (E), Baby Blue (F),
Dark Persian (G), Pure Pink
(H), and Strawberry (I)**

**Size 9/I (5.5-mm) aluminum
crochet hook or size to obtain
gauge**

Yarn needle

Note: Colors used represent
colors we suggest; actual color
names differ with manufacturer or
retailer. Choose colors appropriate to your project.

Directions

Gauge: 1 motif = 7¾" square

To make sure afghan is desired
size, check your gauge.

Size: 55¾" x 55¾"

Note: See page 22 for list of
abbreviations and other general
directions.

Special Stitches

Dc 3 together (dc3tog):
Keeping last lp of each st on hook,
work dc in next 3 sts, yo and draw
through all 4 lps on hook to
make cl.

Tr 3 together (tr3tog):
Keeping last lp of each st on hook,
work tr in next 3 sts, yo and draw
through all 4 lps on hook to
make cl.

Tr 4 together (tr4tog): Work
as for tr3tog, working in next 4 sts,
yo and draw through all 5 lps on
hook to make cl.

Afghan

Work center flower petals of ea
motif in combination (combo) of
1 light color and 1 dark color.
Working light color first and dark
color second, make 17 squares
with D and E (Combo 1),
16 squares with F and G
(Combo 2), and 16 squares with
colors H and I (Combo 3).

First Motif: Work First Motif
in Combo 1 (see above). With C,
ch 6; sl st in beg ch to form ring.

Rnd 1 (rs): Ch 1, work 12 sc
in ring; sl st to beg sc to join:
12 sc.

Rnd 2: Ch 1, working into
front lp only for this rnd, work
2 sc in each sc around; sl st to
beg st: 24 sc. Fasten off.

Rnd 3: With rs facing, join
light color in any rem lp of Rnd 2
with sl st, ch 1, 2 sc in each rem lp
around; sl st in beg sc: 24 sc.

Rnd 4: Ch 4 (counts as first tr),
working in front lps only, tr3tog
over next 3 sts; ★ ch 9, tr4tog
over next 4 sts; rep from ★ 4 more
times, ch 9; sl st to top of beg
ch-4 with A: 6 petals. Fasten off
light color.

Rnd 5: With A, ch 1, sc in
same st; ★ (ch 3, sk 1 ch, sc in
next ch) 4 times, ch 3, sk 1 ch ★★,
sc in top 9 of next petal; rep
from ★ around, ending last rep at
★★; sl st to beg sc: 30 ch-3 lps.

Rnd 6: Sl st to center of next ch-3 lp, ch 1, sc in same lp; ★ ch 3, sc in next lp; rep from ★ around, ending last rep with ch 3, sl st in beg sc.

Rnd 7: Ch 1, sc in same sc as join; ★ (ch 3, sc in next ch-3 lp) 15 times, ch 3 ★★, sc in next sc; rep from ★ once more, ending at ★★, sl st to beg sc: 32 ch-3 lps. Fasten off A.

Rnd 8: Working in rem lps of Rnd 3 behind light-colored petals, join dark color with sl st into lp at center of any petal; ★ ch 6, tr3tog over next 3 sts, working from back to front, sl st around center ch of ch-9 lp of Rnd 4, ch 6, sc in next st; rep from ★ 5 times more; sl st to base of beg ch-6. Fasten off.

Rnd 9: With rs facing, join B with sc in any ch-3 lp of Rnd 7; ★ (ch 3, sc in next ch-3 lp) 4 times, ch 3, sk next lp, in next lp work [dc3tog, ch 3, tr4tog, ch 4, sl st to top of last cl made (picot made), ch 3, dc3tog], ch 3, sk next lp ★★, sc in next lp; rep from ★ around, ending last rep at ★★; sl st to beg sc. Fasten off.

Second Motif: Using Combo 2, work as for First Motif through Rnd 8.

Rnd 9 (Joining Rnd): With rs facing, join B with sc in any ch-3 lp of Rnd 7, (ch 3, sc in next lp) 4 times; ★ ch 3, sk next lp, in next lp work [dc3tog, ch 3, tr4tog, ch 2, sl st in picot of First Motif, ch 2, sl st to top of last cl made (picot made), ch 3, dc3tog], ch 3, sk next lp, sc in next lp ★★, (ch 1, sc into corresponding ch-3 lp of First Square, ch 1, sc in next ch-3 lp) 4 times; rep from ★ to ★★ once more; cont from ★ of Rnd 9 of First Motif to finish rnd.

Rem Motifs of First Afghan Row: Cont making and joining

motifs as for Second Motif, following Assembly Diagram for color combos.

First Motif of Rem Afghan Rows: Following Assembly Diagram, make and join as for Second Motif.

Second–Seventh Motifs of Rem Afghan Rows: Following Assembly Diagram, make and join as for Second Motif, joining two adjacent sides.

Finishing

Edging: With rs facing, join B with sl st in any corner 4-tr cl.

Rnd 1 (rs): Ch 1, sc in same lp, ch 3; ★ (sc in next ch-3 lp, ch 3) 8 times, sc in top of next cl, ch 3, sc in joining of picots, ch 3, sc in top of next cl, ch 3; rep from ★ to next corner; at corner, work sc in picot, ch 3; rep from ★ around entire afghan; sl st to beg sc.

Rnd 2: Sl st to center of next ch-3 lp, sc in same lp, ch 3; ★ sc in next ch-3 lp, ch 3; rep from ★ around; sl st to beg sc.

Rnd 3: Sl st to center of next ch-3 lp, sc in same lp, ch 3; ★ (sc in next ch-3 lp, ch 3) across to corner ch-3 lp, in corner ch-3 lp work [dc3tog, ch 3, tr4tog (ch 4, sl st in top of last cl made for picot), ch 3, dc3tog, ch 3]; rep from ★ around; sl st to beg sc. Fasten off.

Weave in ends on ws.

1	2	3	1	2	3	1
2	3	1	2	3	1	2
3	1	2	3	1	2	3
1	2	3	1	2	3	1
2	3	1	2	3	1	2
3	1	2	3	1	2	3
1	2	3	1	2	3	1

Assembly Diagram

Basic Crochet Directions

Standard Abbreviations

beg	begin(ning)
bet	between
ch	chain(s)
cl	cluster
cont	continue
dc	double crochet
dec	decreas(es) (ed) (ing)
est	established
lp(s)	loop(s)
rem	remain(s) (ing)
rep	repeat(s)
rs	right side
sc	single crochet
sk	skip(ped)
sl st	slip stitch
sp	space
st(s)	stitch(es)
tog	together
tr	treble crochet
ws	wrong side
yo	yarn over

Gauge

Before beginning project, work gauge swatch, using recommended size hook. Count and compare number of stitches per inch in swatch with designer's gauge or finished size of your square with size given as gauge. If you have fewer stitches in your swatch or if your swatch is larger than gauge, try smaller hook. If you have more stitches or your swatch is smaller, try larger hook.

Joining Yarn

To change colors or to begin new skein of yarn at end of row, work last yarn over for last stitch of previous row with new color.

Fastening Off

Cut yarn, leaving 6" tail. Yarn over and pull tail through last loop on hook. Thread tail into large-eyed yarn needle and weave it carefully into back of work.

Mosaic Crackle Box

Materials

Aleene's Enhancers™: All-Purpose Primer, Satin Varnish, Mosaic Crackle Medium, Mosaic Crackle Activator, Clear Gel Medium
Water
Waxed paper
Paintbrushes: sponge, ¾" flat
Wooden box
Sandpaper
Tack cloth
Aleene's Premium-Coat™ Acrylic Paints: Deep Sage, Gold
Palette knife
Aleene's Decoupage Prints and Papers™: Alphabetica Tropical Butterflies
Paper towels

Turn a plain wooden box into an instant heirloom by adding a crackle finish.

Design by Chris Wallace

Directions

1 Mix equal parts primer and water on waxed paper. Apply 1 coat of mixture to box, using sponge brush. Let dry. Sand box smooth. Wipe box with tack cloth to remove any dust.

2 Pour small puddle of each color of paint onto waxed paper. For each, mix 1 part paint with 2 parts Mosaic Crackle Medium. Apply 1 coat of Deep Sage mixture to lid and 1 coat of Gold mixture to box, using sponge brush. Let dry. Then apply 1 coat of Gold mixture to lid and 1 coat of Deep Sage mixture to box, using flat brush. Let dry.

3 Cut out desired motifs from decoupage papers. Working over small area at a time, apply Mosaic Crackle Medium to box where desired, using sponge brush. Press cutout onto glue-covered area. When satisfied with design, apply 1 coat of Mosaic Crackle Medium to cutouts. Let dry. Apply 1 coat of Mosaic Crackle Activator to box and lid, using sponge brush. Let dry.

4 To antique, mix 1 part Deep Sage with 3 parts Clear Gel Medium on waxed paper. Apply mixture sparingly to cutouts, using sponge brush; immediately wipe off excess with paper towel. Let dry.

5 Apply 1 coat of Satin Varnish to box and lid, using sponge brush. Let dry.

Decoupage Table

Picture this: An inexpensive frame and a decoupage print can make an elegant side table.

Materials
Frame with glass and cardboard in desired size
4 wooden legs with screws
Drill with appropriate bit
Aleene's Enhancers™: All-Purpose Primer and Satin Varnish
Fine sandpaper
Tack cloth
Aleene's Premium-Coat™ Acrylic Paints: Dusty Green, colors to match print (if print is smaller than frame)
Assorted paintbrushes
Aleene's Decoupage Print™
Aleene's Tacky Glue™
Hammer and framing brads
4 (4"-lengths) 1" x 1" wooden strips (optional)
8 nails or screws (optional)

Directions
1 Lay frame right side down. Position 1 leg in each corner and mark placement of screws. Drill holes in frame back at marks.

2 Apply 1 coat of primer to frame and each leg. Let dry. Sand each lightly. Wipe frame and each leg with tack cloth to remove any dust. Paint frame and legs Dusty Green. Let dry.

3 Apply 1 coat of varnish to all sides of frame and legs, letting 1 side dry before applying to next side.

4 Cut print and cardboard to fit frame. If frame is larger than print, pounce complementary colors of acrylic paint onto border of print, using various brushes. Let dry.

5 Clean and dry glass. Place glass into frame. Place print wrong side up on glass. Glue print in place. Let dry. Then put cardboard over print, glue in place, and let dry. (To make print removable, do not glue in place.) Tack in place with hammer and framing brads. Screw legs in place.

Note: If glass is held in place using framing brads only, do not place heavy items on table (such as vase shown in photo). Depending on size of frame and legs selected, legs may overlap corners of glass, providing reinforcement so that you can place items on table. Or, working from wrong side of frame, place wooden strips across corners of glass and screw or nail them to frame.

Design by Joan Fee, SCD

PAINTED WINDOW FRAME
Mirror

Use a candle to "age" this window frame. Then discover how easy it is to paint the flowers.

Materials
Window frame with 6 panes
Wood putty
Sandpaper: fine, assorted grits
Tack cloth
Paintbrushes: sponge, #3 round, #5 round
Aleene's Enhancers™: All-Purpose Primer, Satin Varnish, Glazing Medium
Aleene's Premium-Coat™ Acrylic Paints: Deep Sage, Deep Peach, Dusty Mauve, Deep Lavender, Dusty Green, Dusty Fuchsia, Soft Sage, Light Pink, Light Blue, White, Ivory, Yellow Ochre
Candle
Waxed paper
½"-diameter pom-poms
Mirror to fit window frame

Directions

1 Fill in any holes in window frame with wood putty. Let dry. Sand frame smooth. Wipe frame with tack cloth to remove any dust.

2 Apply 1 coat of primer to frame. Let dry. Sand again to remove roughness. Paint all sides of frame Deep Sage, using sponge brush. Let dry.

3 Rub candle on frame in areas where item would show peeling and chipping from aging, such as edges and corners. (Use candle on its side or on its end for more intensity.)

4 Paint frame Ivory, using sponge brush. Let dry. (If you see brushstrokes after first coat, add second coat; streakiness adds to provincial look.)

5 Sand frame, using fine sandpaper. Where wax was used, Ivory comes off easily to reveal Deep Sage underneath. Continue sanding until frame is smooth and worn looking. Wipe frame with tack cloth to remove any dust.

6 Pour small puddle of Dusty Green on waxed paper. Mix with equal part Glazing Medium. Apply glaze to frame; keep it subtle so that floral design will show up. (Add another glaze coat before varnishing if you want deeper glaze.) Let dry.

7 Refer to photo for floral design. (Don't strive for perfection. When you complete floral design, you'll sand it heavily so impression of flowers—not details—becomes focus.) Mix each

color of paint in floral design with 1 part Glazing Medium.

8 Paint upright ovals Soft Sage for bulbs (see photo), using #3 round brush. Add strokes of Dusty Green and Deep Sage while paint is still wet. Let dry. Add strokes to outside edges of bulb, using Dusty Mauve. Add roots, using #3 brush and Dusty Mauve. Let dry.

9 Paint stems and leaves of bulbs Deep Sage. Each leaf style uses variation of comma stroke. Start leaves on left plant at top. Apply pressure in beginning to spread out bristles and to round stroke. As you approach bulb, let up pressure so that leaf narrows and eventually ends at point. Start leaves on right plant at bulb end, beginning at point and flaring out as you apply pressure to brush; return to point as you gently let up pressure near tip. Let dry.

10 For flower cluster on left, dip small pom-pom into Deep Peach and pounce pom-pom on wood. While Deep Peach is still wet, create several 5-petaled flowers, using #3 brush and small comma stroke with Dusty Mauve, Light Pink, Yellow Ochre, and

Top

Right

Bottom

Left

Design by
Connie Glennon-Hall

Ivory (see photo). Don't clean brush between flowers; mix of paints is more interesting. Let dry.

11 For flower cluster on right, dip pom-pom into Light Pink and then dip top of surface that will touch frame into White and bottom into Dusty Fuchsia to create color gradation, with light at top and dark at bottom. Practice on paper until you're satisfied with results. Work your way down flower, painting side blossoms first, using pom-pom. Finish with blossoms in middle so that they appear closer to you. Let dry.

12 Paint spray of leaves, stems, and vines on top, bottom, and window grids. Make leaves on top, using comma stroke and #5 brush for large leaves and #3 brush for small leaves. Beginning at base of each leaf, flare bristles and let up as you approach tip; use Deep Sage for some and Dusty Green for others. Add stems and vines on window grids trailing down to bottom of frame. Make more leaves at bottom of frame. Add tiny leaves all along vine. Let dry.

13 Paint bluebells as desired, using comma stroke and #3 brush. For back petals, paint Deep Lavender bell-shaped flower with 3 comma strokes, each ending in curved point.

Make several groupings of back petals. Wipe brush off and dip in Light Blue. For front petals, paint 2 more petals between first 3 petals. Let dry.

14 Sand frame so that leaves and flowers have scratches in them. The coarser the sandpaper, the more distressed the result, so start with fine sandpaper and move on to coarse if desired. Wipe frame with tack cloth to remove any dust.

15 If desired, apply second glazing to deepen colors. Let dry. Apply 1 coat of varnish to front and sides of frame. Let dry. Add mirror to frame.

Design by Cheryl Ball, SCD

Ribbons and Roses

A little paint turns plain white linens into charming accessories.

Materials

For 1 place mat and 1 napkin:
Masking tape
White place mat and napkin
Cardboard covered with aluminum foil for work surface
Waxed paper
Aleene's Premium-Coat™ Acrylic Paints: Light Fuchsia, Medium Fuchsia, Light Green, Light Blue, Medium Green
Paintbrushes: #12 flat, #8 flat, #6 round, #4 round

Directions

1 **For each,** tape cloth item to cardboard.

2 Pour small puddle of Light Fuchsia onto waxed paper. Mix 1 part paint and 2 parts water. Create flower in each corner by painting wavy swirl, using #8 brush (see photo). Paint flower center, using #8 brush and Medium Fuchsia. Let dry.

3 Pour small puddle of Light Green onto waxed paper. Mix 1 part paint and 2 parts water. Paint large leaves, using #12 brush (see photo). Paint vines and small leaves, using #6 brush. Let dry. Repeat Step 2 to paint flowers on vines, using #4 brush.

4 Pour small puddle of Light Blue onto waxed paper. Mix 1 part paint with 2 parts water. Paint borders as follows, using #8 brush: paint knot first, then loops, and then streamers (see photo). Let dry.

5 Paint veins in leaves, using chisel edge of #12 brush and Medium Green. Let dry.

Harvest Wreath

Celebrate autumn with a wreath made from fresh fruits and vegetables.

Materials:
Hot-glue gun and glue sticks
   (optional)
 Aleene's Thick Designer Tacky
   Glue™
Vegetables and fruits: lemons,
   gourds, green and red apples,
   pears
18"-diameter grapevine wreath
Aleene's Botanical Preserved
   Flowers and Foliage™: fall
   leaves
Dried yarrow
Silk leaves and yellow flowers
5 yards 3"-wide ribbon
Florist's wire

Directions

Randomly glue vegetables and
fruits to wreath as desired. Let dry.
(You can use hot glue for quick
hold until you're satisfied with
placement and then use Tacky
Glue for permanent hold.)

Glue on leaves, yarrow, and
silk flowers to fill. Let dry.

For each bow, cut 36" length
of ribbon. Shape into bow, securing center with wire. Glue bow
to wreath where desired. Let dry.

Design by Ben Franklin Stores

29

Country Curtain Tiebacks

Trace pattern onto Shrink-It, add paint, and heat for tiebacks that are "for the birds."

Materials

280-320 grit sandpaper
Aleene's Opake Shrink-It™ Plastic
Fine-tip permanent black marker
Aleene's Premium-Coat™ Acrylic Paints in desired colors
Assorted paintbrushes
⅛"-diameter hole punch
Aleene's Baking Board™ or non-stick cookie sheet, sprinkled with baby powder
Aleene's Thick Designer Tacky Glue™
Wooden sticks: 2 (4") lengths, 2 (¾") lengths
2 screws (to fit holes on tiebacks)
Curtain
Ice pick
8-ounce bottle

Birdhouse

Bird

Design by Joan Fee, SCD

Directions

1 For birdhouses and birds, sand 1 side of each piece of Shrink-It so that markings will adhere. Be sure to sand both vertically and horizontally.

2 Using black marker, trace patterns twice onto Shrink-It, reversing 1 bird. (Marker ink may run on sanded surface; runs will shrink and disappear during baking.)

3 For each color of paint, thin with water to ink consistency.

Color each design as desired. Cut out designs. For tiebacks, cut 2 (2" x 10¾") pieces of Shrink-It. Punch hole ¼" from 1 end of each tieback.

4 Preheat toaster oven or conventional oven to 275° to 300°. Place designs on Baking Board and bake in oven. Edges should begin to curl within 25 seconds. If not, increase temperature slightly. If edges begin to curl as soon as designs are put in oven, reduce temperature. After about

1 minute, designs will lie flat. Remove designs from oven. While still hot, form non-punched end of each tieback around 8-ounce bottle. Hold in place until hard. Let designs cool.

5 Glue birds to birdhouses; glue birdhouses to tiebacks. Let dry. Glue long stick to back of each birdhouse. For perch, heat ice pick over flame and insert below painted hole. Repeat on second birdhouse. Glue 1 small stick into each hole. Let dry.

Open Swirls Afghan

This crocheted afghan is swirling with creativity.

Materials
3.5 -ounce skeins Caron Dawn Sayelle® acrylic worsted-weight yarn: 15 skeins Aran (A); 3 skeins Light Blue Velvet (B); 2 skeins each Light Wicker Green (C), Pale Terra Cotta (D), and Maize (E); 1 skein each Colonial Blue (F), Medium Wicker Green (G), Terra Cotta (H), and Canary (I)
Size 8/H (5-mm) crochet hook or size to obtain gauge
Yarn needle

Note: Colors used represent colors we suggest. Actual color names differ with retailer or manufacturer. Choose colors appropriate to your project.

Directions
Gauge: In dc, 10 sts = 3"
  11 rows = 4"
Size: Approximately 47" x 70", excluding fringe

Special Stitches
Front post dc (fpdc): Yo, insert hook from front to back to front around post of st below, draw up lp, (yo, draw through 2 lps) twice.

Front post tr (fptr): Yo twice, insert hook from front to back to front around post of st below, draw up lp, (yo, draw through 2 lps) 3 times.

Front post double tr (fpdtr): Yo 3 times, insert hook from front to back to front around post of st below, draw up lp, (yo, draw through 2 lps) 4 times.

Open swirl: Work (fpdc, fptr, and fpdtr) around post of same st from top to bottom; sc in top of same st.

Afghan
Note: To change yarn colors, work last st of current color up through last yo and pull through, drop current color, pick up new color, yo with and draw through both lps on hook with new color.

See page 22 for list of abbreviations and other general directions.

With A, ch 233.
Row 1 (rs): Dc in 4th ch from hook and each ch across; turn. 231 sts.
Rows 2 and 3: Ch 3 (counts as first dc), dc in each st across, changing to B in last st of Row 3; turn. Fasten off A.
Row 4: With B, ch 1, sc in first st and in next 9 dc; ★ open swirl in next st, sc in next 5 sts, open swirl in next st ★★, sc in next 27 sts; rep from ★ across, ending last rep at ★★, sc in last 10 sts, changing to A; turn. Fasten off B.
Row 5: With A, ch 3 (counts as first dc), dc in each sc across, including sc of swirl, changing to F in last st; turn. Fasten off A.

Row 6: With F, ch 1, sc in 13 sts; (open swirl in next st, sc in next 33 sts) 6 times, open swirl in next st, sc in last 13 sts, changing to A in last st; turn. Fasten off F.
Row 7: Rep Row 5, changing to B in last st; turn. Fasten off A.
Row 8: Rep Row 4, changing to A in last st; turn. Fasten off B.
Row 9: Rep Row 5, changing to D in last st; turn. Fasten off A.
Row 10: With D, ch 1, sc in 27 sts; ★ open swirl in next st, sc in next 5 sts, open swirl in next st, sc in next 27 sts; rep from ★ across, changing to A in last st; turn. Fasten off D.
Row 11: Rep Row 5, changing to H in last st; turn. Fasten off A.
Row 12: With H, ch 1, sc in 30 sts, (open swirl in next st, sc in next 33 sts) 5 times, open swirl in next st, sc in last 30 sts, changing to A in last st; turn. Fasten off H.
Row 13: Rep Row 5, changing to D in last st; turn. Fasten off A.
Row 14: Rep Row 10, changing to A in last st; turn. Fasten off D.
Row 15: Rep Row 5, changing to C in last st. Fasten off A.
Row 16: With C, rep Row 4, changing to A in last st. Fasten off C.
Row 17: Rep Row 5, changing to G in last st. Fasten off A.
Row 18: With G, rep Row 6, changing to A in last st. Fasten off G.

Design by Mary Lamb Becker

Row 19: Rep Row 5, changing to C in last st. Fasten off A.

Row 20: With C, rep Row 16, changing to A in last st. Fasten off C.

Row 21: Rep Row 5, changing to E in last st. Fasten off A.

Row 22: With E, rep Row 10, changing to A in last st. Fasten off E.

Row 23: Rep Row 5, changing to I in last st. Fasten off A.

Row 24: With I, rep Row 12, changing to A in last st. Fasten off I.

Row 25: Rep Row 5, changing to E in last st. Fasten off A.

Row 26: With E, rep Row 22, changing to A in last st. Fasten off E.

Row 27: Rep Row 5, changing to B in last st. Fasten off A.

Rep Rows 4–27 4 times more, then rep rows 4–8 once.

Next Row: Rep Row 5; do not fasten off; turn.

Next 2 Rows: Rep Row 2. Fasten off.

Fringe: Fringe both short ends of afghan as follows: Omitting all A rows, use 6 (18") yarn lengths of matching color for each color row. Holding all 6 strands tog, fold in half. Using crochet hook, pull lp of fold from rs to ws through end of row. Insert yarn ends through lp; pull to tighten. Trim fringe ends.

Tulips and Daffodils

Colorful twists of Satin Sheen make a bouquet of daffodils and tulips to brighten your home.

Materials
For each: **Fine-tip permanent marker**
½" flat paintbrush
Paper towels
Blow dryer
12" length stiff wire for each stem
Low-temp glue gun and glue sticks
Green florist's tape
1"-square pop-up craft sponge
6"-diameter terra-cotta pot
Florist's foam
Moss
For tulips: **Aleene's Satin Sheen Twisted Ribbon™: yellow, red, green**
Aleene's Premium-Coat™ Acrylic Paints: Medium Apricot, Dusty Fuchsia
For daffodils: **Aleene's Satin Sheen Twisted Ribbon™: yellow, green**
Aleene's Premium-Coat™ Acrylic Paint: Medium Red

Directions

1 **For tulips,** untwist yellow or red twisted ribbon. For each flower, trace 7 petals onto ribbon, using marker. Cut out just inside traced lines.

2 For yellow tulip, load Medium Apricot onto brush and then dab onto paper towel to remove excess. Paint edges of each petal. For red tulip, brush petals using Dusty Fuchsia. Let dry.

3 To shape petals, heat edges until slightly curled, using blow dryer. (Be sure to heat unpainted side so that petals curl in. Blow dryers vary; test heat first.)

4 For each stamen, cut 1 (2" x 3") piece from yellow twisted ribbon. Cut fringe along 1 end. Wrap stamen around wire; glue in place. Let dry. Wrap with florist's tape. Heat with blow dryer to curl.

5 Glue petals around stamen, overlapping slightly. Let dry. Wrap florist's tape around bottom of petals and along length of wire.

6 **For daffodils,** cut 8" length of yellow twisted ribbon and untwist. Fold twisted ribbon in half along 1 short edge; then fold right side to center bottom. Fold left side to back at center bottom, forming V. Trace daffodil petal onto twisted ribbon and cut out. For each daffodil center, cut 1 (2" x 5") strip. Glue ends of strip together to form cylinder. Let dry.

7 For daffodil stamen, follow Step 4. Brush Medium Red onto center and around base petals. Let dry. Make small hole in center of base petal, using scissors. Slip daffodil onto wire and pull up to stamen. Glue in place. Let dry. Gather bottom of cylinder with your fingers and glue around stamen. Let dry.

8 **For each leaf,** untwist green twisted ribbon. Fold ribbon in half lengthwise and cut desired lengths for leaves, tapering to a point at 1 end. Glue desired size and number of leaves to flower wires or wrap wire with florist tape and glue leaves over wire. Let dry.

9 Dip sponge into same paint used to dry-brush flowers. Dab squares around pot. Let dry.

10 Glue foam into pot. Glue moss to cover foam. Let dry. Insert flowers and leaves into foam.

Tulip Petal

Daffodil Petal

CLASSY CRACKLE

Use metallic foil and a paint-on crackle finish to enrich your home decor.

Materials
Wooden frame and mat or candle or vase
Sandpaper
Tack cloth
Aleene's Enhancers™: All-Purpose Primer, Glazing Medium, Mosaic Crackle Medium, Mosaic Crackle Activator, Satin Varnish
Waxed paper
Aleene's Essentials™: Burgundy, Gold
Paintbrushes: fan, large flat
Aleene's Crafting Foil™: gold, silver
Facial tissue

Directions

1 **For frame,** sand frame smooth. Wipe frame with tack cloth to remove any dust.

2 Mix equal parts primer and water on waxed paper. Apply 1 coat of mixture to frame, using flat brush. Let dry. Apply 1 coat of primer to mat board, using flat brush. Let dry. Then paint mat board Burgundy. Let dry.

3 Apply 1 coat of Mosaic Crackle Medium to mat. When Medium is clear and still tacky, lay desired color foil dull side down on top of mat. Using finger, gently but firmly press foil onto mat. Peel away foil paper. Reapply foil as needed. To protect sheen of foil, use fan brush to apply 1 coat of Glazing Medium over foiled surface. Let dry.

4 Apply 1 coat of Mosaic Crackle Activator over foiled surface. Let dry. Do not force drying time.

5 Paint frame Gold. Let dry. Brush uneven coat of Mosaic Crackle Medium over frame. Let dry. This will result in variety of sizes of cracks. Then apply 1 coat of Burgundy. Let dry. Apply 1 coat of Mosaic Crackle. Let dry. Then apply 1 coat of Mosaic Crackle Activator. Let dry thoroughly at room temperature.

6 **For candle or vase,** cut different-sized triangles from silver foil. Apply 1 coat of Mosaic Crackle Medium to item. When Medium becomes clear and is still tacky, lay silver foil triangles dull side down onto item. Cut gold foil to fill spaces around silver foil triangles and place gold foil. Using finger, gently but firmly press foil onto item. Peel away foil paper. Reapply foil as needed. To protect sheen of foil, use fan brush to apply 1 coat of Glazing Medium over foiled surface. Let dry. Follow Step 4 to activate Crackle Medium.

7 Apply varnish to accessories that will be used outdoors or in high moisture areas, or will be handled frequently. Let dry.

Designs by Inga Johns

Materials

Aleene's Enhancers™: All-Purpose Primer, Satin Varnish
Paintbrushes: #10 flat, stencil, 1" white nylon
Paper towels
Cat and Mouse Pin Pal Kit (See note.)
Sandpaper
Tack cloth
Iron
Fabric to fit shade
Aleene's Thick Designer Tacky Glue™
Wooden craft stick
Wooden lamp with shade
Clothespins
2 yards braid or cording to match fabric
Aleene's Premium-Coat™ Acrylic Paints: Deep Mauve, Deep Green, Ivory, Soft Beige, Dusty Green, Yellow Ochre, Black
Sea sponge
Stencils: circle, triangle
Toothpicks
Fine-tip permanent black marker
Jute
Florist's wire

Note: To order Cat and Mouse Pin Pal Kit, call one heart...one mind at (913) 498-3690.

Directions

1 Apply 1 coat of primer to mouse and each cat. Let dry. Sand mouse and cats smooth. Wipe with tack cloth to remove any dust.

2 For lampshade, iron fabric under at least ¼" at top and bottom edges. Apply glue to top and bottom edges of lampshade, using craft stick. Place bottom of fabric ½" over bottom of shade. Smooth fabric around shade,

SHADY CAT

Here's a purr-fect home accessory for a cat-lover: a stenciled-and-painted lamp.

turning under ¼" where edges meet. Pleat fabric all around top of shade, working with few inches at time and holding in place with clothespins as you work (see photo). Turn bottom edges of fabric to inside, securing with glue. Let dry. Glue braid or cording around top and bottom edges of shade (see photo). Let dry.

3 Referring to photo for color placement, paint lamp base. For center section of lamp base, load sponge with Ivory on 1 side and Soft Beige on other side. Sponge-paint center of lamp base. Let dry. Stencil small triangles as desired, using Deep Green. Dip toothpick into Deep Green and make dots around each triangle. Let dry. Use black marker to draw fish bones (see photo).

4 Paint cats as desired, letting dry between colors. Stencil ears and muzzles, using desired colors. Use black marker to add details to faces and to make dashed lines around each cat body (see photo).

5 For each cat, tear piece of ¼"-wide fabric and knot at center. Glue in place at cat neck. Let dry. Paint button as desired. Let dry. Glue button on top of knot. Let dry.

6 Paint mouse Black. Let dry. Glue jute into hole for mouse tail. Let dry. Glue mouse to side of lamp (see photo). Let dry.

7 Glue 2 cats to lamp base (see photo). Curl wire around pencil (see photo) and glue to remaining cat for cat tail. Let dry. Glue tail to top of lamp shade (see photo). Let dry.

8 Apply 2 coats of Satin Varnish to lamp base and cats, using 1" brush. Let dry.

Design by Chris Wallace

Tissue Flower *Wreath*

Hang this easy project in a window to create a cheerful play of light.

Materials

3 sheets Aleene's Crafting Plastic™
Aleene's Crafting Tissue Paper™:
    yellow, lavender, light fuchsia,
    orange, fuchsia, lime, green
½" flat shader paintbrush
Aleene's Instant Decoupage™ glue:
    Gloss
Lightweight cardboard
Pinking shears
Ultrafine felt-tip permanent black
    marker
Aleene's Thick Designer Tacky
    Glue™
Assorted 1" bright buttons
6"-diameter hoop or desired size

Directions

1 Cut each sheet of Crafting Plastic in half. Cut 1 piece each of yellow, lavender, light fuchsia, orange, and fuchsia tissue paper to fit plastic sheets. For remaining sheet, cut half lime and half green to cover.

2 Working with 1 plastic sheet at a time, brush even, light coat of Instant Decoupage onto 1 side. Lay 1 piece of tissue paper onto covered area. Brush another coat of Instant Decoupage on top. Let dry. Repeat for each color or color combination.

3 Transfer patterns to cardboard and cut out. Trace desired patterns onto tissue side of plastic sheets, using pencil (see photo for colors). Cut out. (Cut some centers with pinking shears, if desired.) Add details to plastic side with marker.

4 Glue flowers together, using Thick Designer Tacky Glue. Let dry.

5 Glue flowers and hearts onto hoop. Let dry. Glue leaves to underside (small leaves at inside). Let dry. Glue on buttons as desired (see photo). Let dry.

Design by Cheryl Ball, SCD

Handmade

Show off your creative talents with this selection of quick and easy gifts to craft.

Page 66

Page 52

Page 55

Page 58

Presents

Padded Photo Albums

Make the outside of your albums as personal as the inside.

Materials

For each: 1 (45" x 60") piece ½"-thick polyester batting

Tape measure

Aleene's Tacky Glue™

Clothespins

1 (22" x 28") sheet white posterboard

For wedding album: 10" x 11½" white photo album

1 yard white moiré fabric

3 yards ¼"-wide white satin ribbon

3 yards 2"-wide iridescent double-ruffled lace

8" x 10" mat frame

⅔ yard ¼"-wide white sequin trim

Florist's wire

Wire cutters

Artificial flower sprays: 1 white sweetheart rose, 1 white lily-of-the-valley

6 florist's picks, each with white tulle and pearls

Aleene's Floral Glue™

For graduation album: 10" x 11½" white photo album

½ yard 45"-wide fabric

Cording: 2 yards ⅜" to match fabric, 1¾ yards ³⁄₁₆" to contrast with fabric

8" x 10" mat frame

Charms or decorative buttons: graduation cap and year

For faithful companion album: 10" x 11½" navy photo album

Fabrics: ½ yard 45"-wide dog print, ⅜ yard 45"-wide plaid

1 yard ⅜"-wide grosgrain ribbon to contrast with fabric

5" x 7" mat frame

Cording: 2 yards ⅜" to match fabric for album, ¾ yard ³⁄₁₆" to match fabric for frame

2 small dog biscuits

Aleene's Instant Decoupage™: matte

Paintbrush

For tapestry album: 10" x 11½" green photo album

Fabrics: ½ yard 54"-wide tapestry, 3" x 14" contrasting strip

2⅛ yards 2"-wide tan curly fringe

1 yard ³⁄₁₆" tan cording

Designs by Rag Shops

Directions for wedding album

1 Remove album pages and set aside. Open album and lay flat on batting. Trace album cover and cut out 1 piece of batting. Using batting as guide, cut 1 piece of fabric, adding 1½" all around. Glue batting to outside cover of album. Center and glue album, batting side down, on wrong side of fabric. Fold excess fabric to inside of album cover and glue, mitering corners. Be sure fabric on front of album is smooth and taut. Use clothespins to hold fabric in place until glue is dry.

2 To make ties, cut 2 (18") lengths of ribbon. Center and glue 1 ribbon length on inside front cover at side edge. Repeat to glue remaining length on inside back cover. Let dry. Cut 1 piece of lace to fit around edges of opened album cover. Glue bound edge of lace around edges on inside of album cover so that lace extends beyond edges of album. Let dry.

3 For inside front cover, cut 1 piece of posterboard, ¼" smaller all around than inside of front album cover. Using posterboard piece as guide, cut 1 piece of fabric, adding 1½" all around. Center and glue posterboard on wrong side of fabric. Fold excess fabric to back of posterboard and glue, mitering corners. With right side up, center and glue covered posterboard on

inside front cover of album, covering cut end of ribbon and bound edge of lace. Use clothespins to hold posterboard in place until glue is dry. Repeat for fabric-covered posterboard on inside back cover.

4 For frame, lay frame on top of remaining batting. Trace frame and cut out 1 piece of batting. Using batting as guide, cut 1 piece of fabric, adding 1½" all around. Glue batting to front of frame. Trim batting from center of frame. Center and glue frame, batting side down, on wrong side of fabric. Cut fabric from inside of frame opening to within 1" of frame. Fold excess fabric to back of frame and glue, mitering corners. Be sure fabric on front of frame is smooth and taut; clip and pleat as needed. Let dry.

5 Cut lace to fit around outside edges of frame. Glue bound edge of lace around frame on back so that lace extends beyond outside edges of frame. Let dry. Glue sequin trim around inside opening on right side of frame. Let dry.

6 Cut remaining satin ribbon in half. Referring to photo, tie each length in bow and secure at center with florist's wire. Cut rose and lily-of-the valley sprays into individual stems; cut stems of tulle picks to 1". Use Floral Glue to attach tulle picks, flowers, and satin bows at bottom left and top right corners of frame. Let dry.

7 Center and glue frame on front cover of album, attaching along sides and bottom only. (Leave top open to insert photo.) Let dry. Replace pages in album.

Directions for graduation album

Follow wedding album directions on pages 44 and 45, using contrasting cording instead of satin ribbon and gluing charms or buttons at frame corners (see photo).

Directions for faithful companion album

Follow wedding album directions on pages 44 and 45, using grosgrain ribbon instead of satin ribbon and cording instead of lace (see photo).

Apply 2 coats of Instant Decoupage to dog biscuits, letting dry between each coat. Glue biscuits to top left and bottom right corners of frame (see photo). Let dry.

Directions for tapestry album

1 Follow steps 1 and 2 of wedding album directions on page 44 to cover album. Fold each long edge of contrasting fabric under ½" and press. Cut 2" length of fringe and glue around center of fabric strip (see photo). Let dry.

Position fabric strip on left side of album front cover and glue top and bottom to inside cover. Let dry.

2 For ties, cut 18" length of cording and tie overhand knot on 1 end. Center and glue untied end on inside front cover at side edge. Let dry. Repeat for back cover.

3 Cut 1 piece of curly fringe to fit around edges of opened album cover. Glue bound edge of curly fringe around edges on inside of album cover so that fringe extends beyond edges of album. Let dry. Follow Step 3 of wedding album directions on pages 44 and 45 to complete tapestry album.

Mini Loaf Tins

Create containers that are almost as enticing as the homemade baked goods you put into them.

Materials

For each: Vinegar
Sandpaper
Tack cloth
Aleene's Enhancers™: All-Purpose Primer
Waxed paper
Paper towels
¾" flat paintbrush
Aleene's Thick Designer Tacky Glue™
Foil loaf pan
Aleene's Tissue Paper™ in desired colors
For gingerbread loaf pan: Mini loaf pan
Aleene's Premium-Coat™ Acrylic Paints: Ivory, Deep Mauve, Beige, Burnt Umber, Black, White
Paintbrushes: stencil, spatter
Checks stencil
Toothpicks
Wooden cutouts: 2 gingerbread people, 1 small heart
Drill or hammer and large nail
24-gauge wire
Wire cutters
Needlenose pliers
For quilt loaf pan: Mini loaf pan
Aleene's Premium-Coat™ Acrylic Paints: Deep Mauve, Yellow Ochre, Deep Violet, Deep Green, Black

#10 flat paintbrush
Toothpicks
For Christmas tree loaf pan: Mini loaf pan
Aleene's Premium-Coat™ Acrylic Paints: Beige, Deep Mauve, Burnt Umber, Deep Green
Pop-up craft sponge
Paintbrushes: ¼" rake, spatter
For foil Christmas tree loaf pan: Aleene's Premium-Coat™ Acrylic Paints: Beige, Deep Mauve, Burnt Umber, Deep Green
Paintbrushes: ¼" rake, spatter
1 wooden Christmas tree
Pop-up craft sponge
For gift tag or recipe card: Posterboard
Tissue paper
For snowman tag holder: Aleene's Premium-Coat™ Acrylic Paints: Ivory, Deep Violet, Deep Green, Black, Deep Mauve
1 wooden snowman
Toothpicks
#1 liner paintbrush
Drill or hammer and large nail
24-gauge wire
Wire cutters
Jute twine

Directions

1 **For each,** wash mini loaf pan in vinegar and water to remove all oil. Let dry. Sand outside of pan. Wipe pan with tack cloth to remove any dust. Apply primer to outside of pan. Let dry.

2 **For gingerbread loaf pan,** paint outside of pan Ivory. Let dry. Paint rim of pan Deep Mauve. Let dry. Paint checks, using stencil and Beige. Let dry. Make dots between checks, using toothpick and Deep Mauve. Let dry.

3 Paint each gingerbread person Burnt Umber. Let dry. Lightly sand edges. Wipe shapes with tack cloth to remove dust. Dot on eyes, using toothpick and Black. Paint squiggly lines around edges, using liner brush and White (see photo). Let dry. Paint heart Deep Mauve. Let dry. Spatter-paint heart with Burnt Umber. Let dry.

4 Make hole in right arm of 1 gingerbread person, in left arm of remaining gingerbread person, and in each side of heart, using drill or hammer and nail. Thread wire lengths through holes to attach shapes, using needlenose pliers to twist wire to secure. Center and glue shapes to 1 side of pan. Let dry.

5 **For quilt loaf pan,** paint pan Deep Mauve. Let dry. Paint rim Deep Violet. Let dry. Paint quilt squares, using flat brush, Yellow Ochre, Deep Violet, and Deep Green (see photo). Let dry.

Designs by Bonnie Stephens

Decorate each quilt square, using liner brush, toothpicks, Yellow Ochre, and Black. Let dry.

6 **For Christmas tree loaf pan,** paint pan Beige. Let dry. Paint rim of pan Deep Mauve. Let dry. Using rake brush and Deep Mauve, paint lines (see photo). Spatter-paint pan with Burnt Umber. Let dry. From sponge, cut small triangle for tree and small rectangle for trunk. Dip sponge shapes into water to expand and wring out excess water. Pour puddles of Deep Green and Burnt Umber onto waxed paper. Dip triangular sponge into Deep Green and blot excess onto paper towels. Press sponge onto pan as desired to paint trees. Repeat with rectangle dipped in Burnt Umber to sponge-paint trunks. Let dry. Paint wooden tree, using Deep Green for main part and Burnt Umber for trunk. Let dry. Lightly sand edges. Wipe tree with tack cloth to remove any dust. Center and glue tree on 1 side of pan. Let dry.

7 **For foil Christmas tree loaf pan,** paint pan Beige; do not paint rim or inside. Let dry. Using rake brush and Deep Mauve, paint lines (see photo). Spatter-paint pan with Burnt Umber. Let dry. From sponge, cut small triangle for tree and small rectangle for trunk. Dip sponge shapes into water to expand and wring out excess water. Pour puddles of Deep Green and Burnt Umber onto waxed paper. Dip triangular sponge into Deep Green and blot excess onto paper towels. Press sponge on pan as desired to paint trees. Repeat with rectangle dipped in Burnt Umber to sponge-paint trunks. Let dry. Bread may be baked as desired in decorated pan.

8 **For each mini loaf pan,** bake desired bread in deco-rated or undecorated foil loaf pan. Let cool. Line mini loaf pan with tissue. Place foil loaf pan with bread on top of tissue.

9 **For gift tags and recipe cards,** use posterboard and tissue paper (see photo). **For snowman tag holder,** paint snowman Ivory and hat Deep Violet. Let dry. Lightly sand edges. Wipe shape with tack cloth to remove any dust. Paint scarf, using liner brush and Deep Green. Dot on eyes and buttons, using toothpicks and Black. For cheeks, load liner brush with small amount of Deep Mauve and apply in circular motion. For nose, load liner brush with Deep Mauve and make squiggle for carrot. Let dry. Make hole in bottom center of snowman, using drill or hammer and nail. Glue desired length of wire into hole. Let dry. Tie jute twine around wire just below snowman and use to hold tag.

Whoa!

Horsing around has never been more fun than with this Satin Sheen stallion.

Materials

Broomstick, closet pole, or
    36" length 1"-diameter dowel
Aleene's Premium-Coat™ Acrylic
    Paint in desired color (optional)
#12 shader paintbrush
Aleene's Enhancers™: Gloss Varnish
Bright blue adult-sized sock
Fiberfill
Hot-glue gun and glue sticks
Aleene's Satin Sheen Twisted
    Ribbon™: 1 yard yellow, 2
    yards each orange and white,
    6 yards red
2 each ¾" and 1" red buttons
2 wiggle eyes

Directions

1 If using dowel or closet pole, paint with desired color. Let dry. Apply 1 coat of varnish. Let dry. (Broom handles are usually painted; just cut to desired length.)

2 Stuff sock firmly with fiberfill. Insert pole into sock up to heel. Shape head, bending at heel for neck (see photo). Glue cuff of sock to pole. Let dry.

3 Untwist yellow twisted ribbon and cut into 2 (1"-wide) pieces. Wrap 1 piece around nose of horse to give shape to head (see photo). Trim ends and glue in place. Wrap remaining piece around upper head and glue in place (see photo). Trim ends. Let dry.

4 For reins, untwist orange twisted ribbon and cut into 2 (1½"-wide) pieces. Knot 1 orange piece to yellow piece along 1 side (see photo). Wrap orange piece around second yellow piece and bring to bottom of sock at back. Repeat on other side so that orange pieces meet at bottom of sock. Wrap orange pieces around sock several times and tie in knot. Trim ends.

5 For mane, untwist red twisted ribbon and cut into 11 (10"-wide) pieces. Knot center of each piece. Fold 1 piece in half and glue together at knot. Let dry. Glue piece to sock heel for bangs. Glue remaining knotted sections to sock heel so that pieces hang down neck of horse. Let dry. To form bangs and mane, tear ribbon into ½"-wide strips (see photo). Trim to desired length.

6 Referring to photo, draw ear and inner ear shapes on yellow and orange ribbon. Cut out. Glue 1 inner ear to each ear. Let dry. Glue ears to head, holding pieces in place until glue sets. Let dry. Glue ¾" buttons in place for nostrils and 1" buttons where orange piece wraps around yellow piece at each side (see photo). Let dry. Glue wiggle eyes in place on head. Let dry.

7 Untwist white twisted ribbon and cut into 2 (2½"-wide) pieces. Tie 1 piece around base of sock. Loop other piece back and forth to make bow. Tie bow in place, using white piece at sock base (see photo). Trim ends.

Design by Cheryl Ball, SCD

Charming Cards

Personalize your greetings with rubber stamps and fusible web.

Materials

For each: Aleene's Crafting Tissue™ in desired colors and patterns
Aleene's Fusible Web™
Card stock
Paper crimper
Deckle-edged scissors (optional)
5" x 6⅞" card with matching envelope
Rubber stamps
Gold pigment ink
Gold embossing powder
Aleene's Tacky Glue™
⅛" hole punch
Assorted charms
Needle and gold thread

Directions for 1 card

Note: See page 5 for tips on working with fusible web.

1 Cut small strips of tissue paper. Crumple each strip and then flatten it, leaving some wrinkles. Iron fusible web to back of each piece of tissue. Fuse tissue pieces to card stock. Cut tissue-covered card stock pieces into 2"-wide strips. Run solid-colored tissue-covered card stock through paper crimper. Cut into desired shapes. Cut patterned tissue-covered card stock with deckle-edge scissors, if desired.

2 Apply desired saying, using rubber stamp and pigment ink. Apply embossing powder. When satisfied with arrangement, glue tissue pieces to card. Punch 2 holes ⅛" apart on bottom of decorative tissue. Tie on charm through holes, using needle and gold thread.

Designs by Lauren Johnston

51

Sheer Secrets

Tuck away treasures in the no-sew pockets of these elegant pillows.

Materials

Sheer fabric (See Step 1 for yardage.)
Decorative pillow
Flat braided trim
Aleene's Fusible Web™
Aleene's Thick Designer Tacky Glue™
1 yard satin ribbon, cut in half
Straight pins

Directions

Note: See page 5 for tips on working with fusible web.

1 Cut sheer fabric 3" or 4" smaller than pillow. Cut 2 pieces of trim to fit along 1 edge of sheer fabric. Glue 1 piece of trim to edge on right side of fabric. Let dry. Set remaining piece of trim aside. Cut fusible web into 3 (¾"-wide) strips. Fuse 1 strip to each undecorated edge on wrong side of sheer fabric. Fuse sheer fabric pocket to center of pillow on 1 side.

2 Glue set-aside trim to pillow above pocket opening (see photo). Before glue dries, insert 1 end of 1 ribbon under trim at center; glue in place (see photo). Glue other length of ribbon to inside center of pocket top. Let dry.

3 Cut piece of trim to fit from top left corner of glued-on trim, around undecorated pocket edges, and up to opposite corner of glued-on trim, plus 1". Glue along untrimmed edges of pocket, folding each cut end under ½". Pin in place until dry.

Design by Darsee Lett and Pattie Donham

Elegant Gift Bags

Turn white bags into practical mementos.

Materials

For each: **White gift bag**
Tulip® Pearl® Dimensional Paint: white
Aleene's Original Tacky Glue™
For bag with invitation: **Wedding invitation**
4 yards 1"-wide white satin ribbon
10" square satin fabric
White trim
White silk flowers
For bag with flap: **White satin fabric triangle (Long edge should be equal to bag width; then add 1" at base for flap.)**
Liquid ravel preventer
Waxed paper
1" sponge paintbrush
3 yards ½"-wide white organdy ribbon
Desired charm

Directions

1 **For bag with invitation,** cut scallops along top edge of bag. Lay bag flat. Squeeze dots of dimensional paint along scalloped edge. Let dry. Repeat on other side of bag.

2 Round corners on invitation. Cut 1 piece of satin ribbon to fit around invitation and glue to edges; or decorate invitation with dimensional paint. Let dry. Center and glue invitation on fabric square. Let dry. Trim fabric to within 1" of invitation. Glue fabric to front of bag where desired. Let dry. Cut 1 piece of white trim to fit around fabric border on invitation; glue trim in place. Let dry. Decorate bag front with swirls of dimensional paint. Let dry.

3 Gather bundle of silk flowers and tie with small piece of ribbon. Glue to bottom right corner of invitation. Let dry. Glue smaller bundle of flowers to top left corner of invitation. Let dry. Wrap bag handles with remaining ribbon. Glue ends in place. Let dry.

4 **For bag with flap,** finish raw edges of fabric triangle with liquid ravel preventer. Let dry. Press flap under ½". Glue flap to inside of bag (see photo). Let dry. Lay bag flat. Paint row of dots along edges of flap and randomly on flap, using dimensional paint (see photo). Let dry.

5 Squeeze puddle of dimensional paint onto waxed paper. Paint plaid pattern on front of bag, using sponge brush (see photo). Squeeze dots of dimensional paint onto bag as desired. Let dry. Tie organdy ribbon in bow and glue to point of flap. Let dry. Glue charm to bow. Let dry.

Designs by Cheryl Ball, SCD

Don't Forget!

Simple wooden shapes dressed up with fused fabric decorate this handy organizer.

Materials
Aleene's Fusible Web™
Assorted fabric scraps (See photo.)
Wooden cutouts: 6 (½"-long)
   teardrops, 5 (½"-diameter)
   circles, 5 (¼"-diameter) circles,
   1 (2") square
Press cloth
Aleene's Thick Designer Tacky
   Glue™
Picket-fence basket
Aleene's Premium-Coat™ Acrylic
   Paint: Yellow Ochre
#12 shader paintbrush
Fine-tip permanent black marker
Toothpick
Aleene's Satin Sheen Twisted
   Ribbon™: beige

Directions
Note: See page 5 for tips on working with fusible web.

1 Iron fusible web to back of fabric scraps. Cut 5 (⅟₁₆"- to ⅛"-wide) strips in various lengths from green fabric for stems. Set aside. For leaves, remove paper backing from remaining green fabric and place wooden teardrops on fusible-web side of fabric, leaving approximately ¼" between pieces. Iron for 10 seconds. (Use press cloth to protect your iron from fusible web residue.) Cut out teardrops, leaving ⅛" around wooden shapes.

2 Remove paper backing from flower fabrics. Place large wooden circles on fusible-web side of fabrics, leaving approximately ¼" between pieces. Iron for 10 seconds, using press cloth. Cut out circles in wavy manner, leaving ⅛" around circles (see photo). Fuse stems to front of basket. Glue flowers and leaves on basket (see photo). Let dry.

3 Paint small wooden circles Yellow Ochre. Let dry. Glue circles to flower centers. Let dry. For sign, fuse 2" wooden square to 2" fabric square. Write DON'T FORGET on sign, using marker. Glue toothpick to back of wooden square. Let dry. Glue sign to basket (see photo). Let dry.

4 Untwist 36"-long piece of twisted ribbon. Tear ribbon into ⅛"- to ¼"-wide strips. Holding several strips together, tie strips in bow. Glue bow to basket handle. Let dry.

Design by Joan Fee, SCD

The Sporting Life

You won't have to fish for compliments when you give your favorite sports fan one of these sophisticated boxes.

Designs by Judy Malone

Materials

For each: Aleene's Enhancers™: All-Purpose Primer, Mosaic Crackle Medium, Mosaic Crackle Activator, Matte Varnish
Paintbrushes: ¾" flat, ½" rake, spatter, #0 liner
Papier-mâché or wooden box
Aleene's Premium-Coat™ Acrylic Paint: Black
Aleene's Thick Designer Tacky Glue™
For fishing box: Aleene's Premium-Coat™ Acrylic Paints: Deep Khaki, Dusty Khaki, Soft Sand
Wire cutters
Fishing lures: 7" Finnish minnow, 2 shiny
Ice pick
Fishing line
2 fishing flies
For golfing box: Aleene's Premium-Coat™ Acrylic Paints: Deep Spruce, Dusty Spruce, Soft Spruce
Golf ball
3 golf tees

Directions

1 **For fishing box,** apply 1 coat of primer to inside and outside of box, using flat brush. Let dry. Paint inside and outside of box with 1 coat of Deep Khaki. Let dry.

2 For outside box lid, with flat brush, apply 1 coat of Crackle Medium. Let dry. Then paint with 1 coat of Dusty Khaki. Let dry. Apply 1 coat of Crackle Activator.

Let dry. To create plaid pattern, paint Deep Khaki stripes in both directions (see photo). Let dry. Paint Soft Sand stripes down middle of Deep Khaki stripes, using rake brush. Let dry. Spatter-paint box lid with Black, using spatter brush. Let dry. Apply 1 coat of varnish to entire box and lid, using flat brush.

3 Use wire cutters to remove barbs from hooks on lures.

Put glue on ends of hooks where you removed barbs. Let dry. Position lures on lid as desired. Punch holes with ice pick and attach lures to lid, using fishing line. Glue on flies. Let dry.

4 **For golfing box,** repeat steps 1 and 2, using Deep Spruce for box, Dusty Spruce for lid and main stripes, and Soft Spruce for accent stripes. Glue ball and tees to top of box lid. Let dry.

Falling for Florals

Dress up your home with an easy three-dimensional wall plaque or floral waterfall.

Wall Plaque

Materials

Aleene's Crafting Plastic™

Felt-tip permanent black marker

Moss

Aleene's Thin-Bodied Glue™

Large zip-top plastic bag

2 (2"-long) twigs

Watercolor paper (130 pound or heavier)

Aleene's Premium-Coat™ Acrylic Paints in desired color (optional)

½" flat paintbrush (optional)

Waxed paper (optional)

Colored card stock or construction paper to match ribbon and flowers

30" length ⅝"-wide wire-edged ribbon

Aleene's Thick Designer Tacky Glue™

Cardboard

Aleene's Botanical Preserved Flowers and Foliage™: dusty rose gypsophila

Bee-shaped charm or decorative button

Directions

1 From Crafting Plastic, cut 2¼"-diameter circle for topiary top, 3"-diameter circle for topiary middle, and 2¼"-tall pot that is 3" wide at top and tapers to 2" wide at bottom (see photo on page 59).

2 Mix moss and Thin-Bodied Glue in zip-top plastic bag. Mold moss onto cutouts. (Wash hands frequently because they will get sticky.) While moss is still wet, glue twigs between cutouts, positioning moss under and on top of twigs (see photo). Let dry at least 24 hours.

3 Tear piece of watercolor paper about 1" larger all around than widest part of topiary design (see photo). Leave watercolor paper natural or, if desired, pour small amount of paint onto waxed paper, mix 1 part paint with 2 parts water, paint evenly onto paper, and let dry.

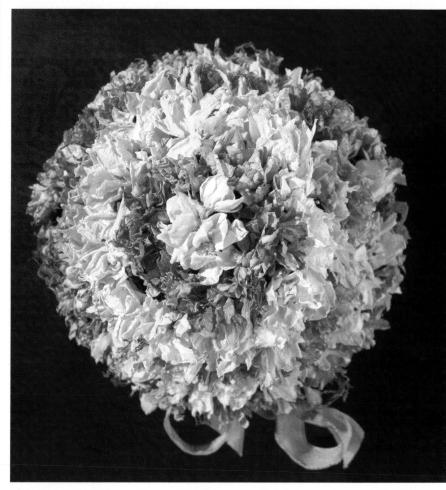

Designs by Lauren Johnston and Lori Thompson

When viewed from above, the floral waterfall looks like a bouquet.

4 Cut 1 piece of colored card stock about ½" larger all around than watercolor paper. For hanger, cut 8" length of ribbon. Glue ends to back of card stock to form loop, using Tacky Glue (see photo). Let dry. Center and glue watercolor paper on card stock. Let dry. Glue cardboard to back of colored stock. Let dry.

5 Center and glue moss design on watercolor paper, using Tacky Glue. Let dry. Glue gypsophila into moss as desired and glue on bee charm or button. Let dry. Tie remaining ribbon in bow and glue at center rim of pot. Let dry.

Floral Waterfall

Materials
For each: **Terra-cotta pots: 1 each in 5½"-, 3½"-, and 2¼"-diameter**
Florist's foam
Aleene's Thick Designer Tacky Glue™
Moss
Aleene's Botanical Preserved Flowers and Foliage™: delphinium, gypsophila, lavendula, or desired flowers
Aleene's Floral Glue™
½ yard ⅝"-wide wire-edged ribbon (optional)

Directions for 1 floral waterfall

Glue foam into each pot, using Tacky Glue. Let dry. Glue medium pot to center of foam in large pot. Let dry. Glue small pot to center of foam in medium pot. Let dry. Glue moss to cover foam in all pots. Let dry. Glue flowers in moss as desired, using Floral Glue. Let dry. If desired, tie ribbon in bow around large pot.

59

The Look of Leather

Achieve this rich finish for just pennies, using paper and glue.

Materials

For each: Ruler
Posterboard
Tracing paper
Aleene's Fabric Stiffener™
Aleene's Thick Designer Tacky
   Glue™
Aleene's Premium-Coat™ Acrylic
   Paints: Deep Beige, Black, Burnt
   Umber, Burgundy (optional)
Aleene's Enhancers™: Glazing
   Medium, Matte Varnish
Waxed paper
Paintbrushes: ¾" flat, sponge
Cloth
Brass corners and charm (optional)
For folder: 1 yard wire-edged
   ribbon
For each box: Aleene's Boxmaker™
   in desired size

Directions

1 **For folder,** cut 1 (11" x 15") piece of posterboard. Measure and mark 2½" from 1 long edge, 5" from left side, and 4" from right side. Cut 2½" x 5" rectangle from bottom left and 2½" x 4" rectangle from bottom right. Fold up flap along marked lines.

2 Using posterboard piece as guide, cut piece of tracing paper ½" larger all around than posterboard. Crumple tracing paper and then flatten it, leaving some wrinkles. Apply fabric stiffener to 1 side of posterboard and to within ½" of edges on 1 side of wrinkled tracing paper. With fabric stiffener sides together, center posterboard on wrinkled tracing paper. Working from center outward, push bubbles out of tracing paper. Let dry. Repeat to cover other side of posterboard. Tear edges of tracing paper even with posterboard.

3 Mix 1 part Deep Beige with 3 parts Glazing Medium on waxed paper. Paint mixture over each side of tracing paper, letting 1 side dry before turning over. Mix 1 part Black, 2 parts Burnt Umber, and 6 parts Glazing Medium on waxed paper. Working on 1 side and small area at a time, paint on Burnt Umber mixture. Wipe off in circular motion, using cloth. Let color remain in paper creases. Let dry. Apply 1 coat of varnish to each side, letting 1 side dry before turning over.

4 Apply Glazing Medium to brass corners and charm for antique finish. Wipe off, using cloth. Let dry. Glue corners on front flap; glue charm where desired. Let dry. Glue center of ribbon to center back of folder. Let dry. Fold to close. Tie ribbon in bow at front.

5 **For each box,** follow steps 2 and 3 to cover box form and to apply faux leather finish to box. (Small box in photo was painted with mixture of Burgundy and Glazing Medium for first coat and Black and Glazing Medium for top coat.) Referring to manufacturer's directions, assemble box lid and bottom. Apply 1 coat of Glazing Medium to brass corners and charm for antique finish. Wipe off, using cloth. Let dry. Glue on brass corners and charm (if desired). Let dry.

Designs by Judy Malone

Designs by Mary Jane Mooney

Fancy Foiling

Decoupage papers and craft foil turn ordinary glass bottles into special accessories for a vanity.

Materials

For each: **Aleene's Decoupage Prints™ in desired pattern**
Aleene's Instant Decoupage™
1"-wide sponge paintbrush
Glass bottle
Kitchen sponge
Aleene's 3-D Foiling Glue™
Aleene's Gold Crafting Foil™
Desired embellishments

Directions for 1 bottle

1 Cut out desired design from decoupage paper, trimming close to edge of design. Apply Instant Decoupage to back of cutout, using sponge brush. Place cutout on bottle where desired. To remove bubbles, wet kitchen sponge and press gently from center of cutout to outside edges. Clean any Instant Decoupage residue from bottle.

2 Apply Foiling Glue to outer edge of cutout and where desired on bottle. Let dry for 12 hours. (Glue will be sticky when dry. Glue must be thoroughly dry before foil is applied.) To apply foil, lay foil dull side down on top of glue lines. Using finger, press foil onto glue, completely covering glue with foil. Peel away foil paper. Decorate bottle as desired with embellishments.

61

❖Wooden Quilt❖

Make a lasting heirloom from precut shapes.

Materials

Wooden cutouts: 32 large, 16 medium, and 28 small triangles; 16 large rectangles; 6 medium and 8 small diamonds; 4 medium squares
Acrylic paints: burgundy, dusty mauve, white, meadow green, hunter green
Paintbrushes: ½" flat, sponge
Matte acrylic spray sealer
Paper plate
16" x 20" piece white mat board
Sea sponge
Tablespoon
Paper towels
Aleene's Thick Designer Tacky Glue™
16" x 20" precut mat with 11" x 14" opening
Piece of cardboard
16" x 20" unfinished wooden frame with hanging hardware
Fine sandpaper
Tack cloth
Ruler
Silicone glue
Toothpick (optional)

Directions

1 Using flat brush and letting dry between coats, apply 2 coats of paint to wooden cutouts as follows: 8 large triangles, 8 small diamonds, and 4 large rectangles with burgundy; 8 large triangles, 6 medium diamonds, and 8 large rectangles with dusty mauve; 8 large triangles, 4 medium triangles, and 4 large rectangles with white; 8 large triangles and 2 medium squares with meadow green; and 12 medium triangles, 28 small triangles, and 2 medium squares with hunter green. Spray light coat of acrylic sealer over all pieces. Let dry.

2 Mix 1 tablespoon white with 2 tablespoons dusty mauve on paper plate. Use sponge brush to apply 2 coats to mat board, letting dry between coats. Pour quarter-sized dot of white paint on paper plate. Dip damp sea sponge into paint and dab onto paper towel to remove excess paint. Sponge-paint mat board. Let dry. Spray mat board with acrylic sealer. Let dry.

3 Squeeze craft glue onto wrong side of precut mat, using piece of cardboard as squeegee to spread glue evenly. Position mat on top of painted mat board, aligning outside edges; press firmly in place. Cover with weighted object to keep flat. Let dry.

4 Lightly sand frame. Wipe frame with tack cloth to remove dust. Apply 2 coats of dusty mauve, using sponge brush and letting dry between coats. Spray with light coat of sealer. Let dry.

5 To find center of pink mat board, place ruler from 1 corner to diagonal corner; lightly draw short line at center, using pencil. Repeat with opposite diagonal corners to make small X at center.

6 Lightly sand bottoms of wooden cutouts near edges to make sure pieces lie flat. (Take care not to sand off edges.) Wipe cutouts with tack cloth to remove dust. Align center of green squares with center mark on mat (see photo). Glue in place, spreading backs of pieces with small amount of silicone glue. Continue gluing wooden cutouts in place, 1 at a time, referring to photo for design. (Silicone glue lets you reposition pieces as needed until glue dries, in about 1 hour.) While glue dries, check periodically to be sure pieces do not slide out of place. If glue oozes onto board, remove it, using toothpick either before or after glue dries.

7 For top border on mat, lightly draw line ¼" from beveled edge, extending 3" beyond corners. Measure and mark top center of line. Glue large diamond flower motif at center (see photo). Glue 1 flower motif at each corner. Measure and mark halfway between center motif and each corner motif; glue small flower motifs on marks. Repeat to glue flowers along bottom border of mat. For small flower motifs at sides, measure distance from 1 top corner to small flower on top border. Using this measurement, measure and mark down from top along sides and glue small flowers at marks. Let dry about 1 hour. Carefully erase pencil lines. Place completed project into frame and secure. Attach hanging hardware.

Design by Cindy Groom Harry® for Ben Franklin Stores

Whirligig

This child's toy is a breeze to make with Shrink-It Plastic.

Design by Denise Morgan

Materials

For each: Aleene's Shrink-It™
    Plastic
Sandpaper
Felt-tip permanent marker
Kitchen sponge
Aleene's Premium-Coat™ Acrylic
    Paint in desired color
Aleene's Enhancers™: Gloss Varnish
Hole punch or craft knife
Aleene's Thick Designer Tacky
    Glue™
Golf tee
2" button
Bendable drinking straw

Directions for 1 whirligig

1 Sand both sides of Shrink-It so that markings and paint will adhere. Be sure to sand thoroughly both horizontally and vertically. Lay Shrink-It on top of pattern. Using marker, trace pattern twice onto Shrink-It. Cut out.

2 Sponge-paint both sides of 1 piece in desired color, letting 1 side dry before turning over. Repeat to brush varnish on each side of piece.

3 Referring to pattern, punch holes on each Shrink-It piece where indicated. Place unpainted piece behind painted piece, matching holes but offsetting 2 tabs so that pieces interlock. Glue centers together. Let dry.

4 Working from front to back, place each hole-punched tab onto golf tee, 1 hole at a time (see photo). Push tee firmly through center hole when you have added all tabs. Glue button to top of tee. Let dry. Place tee into top of straw. Bend straw down at flexible joint to form handle.

Dad's Message Organizer

This no-sew organizing center offers Dad an attractive place for those small items that clutter his desk or dresser.

Directions

Note: See page 5 for tips on working with fusible web.

1 From fusible web, cut 1 (4" x 24") piece and 1 (16" x 24") piece for inside pocket; then cut 1 (3" x 22") piece and 1 (16" x 22") piece for outside pocket.

2 From solid fabrics, cut 1 (20" x 24") piece for inside pocket, 1 (19" x 22") piece for outside pocket, and 1 (14" x 18") piece for backing.

3 Center board on wrong side of print fabric piece. Fold and glue excess fabric to back of foam-core board. Trim corners as shown in Diagram 1. Stick pins into fabric to hold in place until it will stay on its own. (Do not leave pins in glue until it dries because pins will be hard to remove.) Let dry.

4 For pockets, fuse web pieces to wrong side of fabric pieces (see Diagrams 2 and 3). Remove paper backing. With fusible sides together, fold inside pocket in half vertically to measure 12" x 20" and fuse. With fusible sides together, fold outside pocket in half

horizontally to measure 9½" x 22" and fuse.

5 Place folded edge of inside pocket 9" from top of board, with 3" extending beyond each side of board. Fold and glue excess fabric to back of board. Let dry. Repeat with outside pocket, placing top edge 3½" below top edge of inside pocket and extending 4" beyond each side of board.

6 Apply glue close to edges on back of board. Place wrong side of fabric backing over glue. Let dry. Cut 1 piece of gimp to fit around edges of board. Beginning at bottom of board, glue gimp along outside edges. Let dry.

7 Referring to Diagram 1, glue remaining gimp to back of board to form hanger. Let dry.

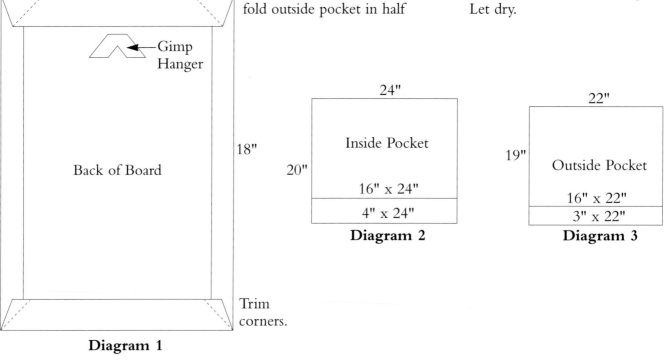

14"

Gimp Hanger

Back of Board

18"

Trim corners.

Diagram 1

24"

Inside Pocket

20"

16" x 24"

4" x 24"

Diagram 2

22"

Outside Pocket

19"

16" x 22"

3" x 22"

Diagram 3

Design by Hancock Fabrics

Pet Presents

These treats for your favorite pet—or pet-lover—are doggone easy!

Materials

For collar or ribbon: Fabric collar or ribbon

Aleene's Premium-Coat™ Acrylic Paints: Holiday Red or Black

Small paintbrush

For rhinestone jar: Red acrylic jewels: 4 (6½-mm) and 1 (10-mm) for each paw

Aleene's Jewel-It™ Glue or Aleene's Thick Designer Tacky Glue™

Glass jar

For painted jar: Dog paw and bone stencils

Glass jar

Felt-tip permanent marker: black or red

Aleene's Premium-Coat™ Acrylic Paints: Holiday Red, Black

Aleene's Enhancers™: Clear Gel Medium

Waxed paper

Palette knife or toothpick

Small paintbrush

For 3-D foiling jar: Paw stencil

Glass jar

Felt-tip permanent gold marker

Aleene's 3-D Foiling Glue™

Aleene's Gold Crafting Foil™

Directions for collar or ribbon

Decorate collar or ribbon with freehand dog paws and bones, using undiluted paint (see photo). Let dry.

Directions for rhinestone jar

For each paw, glue on 1 (10-mm) jewel for pad and 4 (6½-mm) jewels for toes. Apply glue to back of each jewel and gently press jewel onto jar where desired. Be sure to use enough glue so that glue comes up around sides of jewel. (Glue will dry clear.) Repeat as desired, letting 1 side of jar dry at least 2 hours before working on remaining side. Let finished jar dry at least 2 hours before using.

Directions for painted jar

Trace stencil onto jar as many times as desired, using black or red marker. Pour puddle of matching paint color onto waxed paper. Mix 3 parts paint and 1 part Gel Medium, using palette knife or toothpick. Paint over and inside traced lines. Let dry.

Directions for 3-D foiling jar

Trace stencil onto jar as many times as desired, using gold marker. Working on small area at a time, fill in traced areas with 3-D Foiling Glue, letting dry at least 1 hour before applying to next section. (Do not place jar on its side; tilt it so that glue does not run or stick.) When finished filling in paw prints, let jar dry 12 to 24 hours. (Glue will be sticky when dry. Glue must be thoroughly dry before you apply foil.) To apply gold foil to each paw print, lay foil dull side down on top of glue-covered area. Using finger, press foil onto glue, completely covering glue with foil. Peel away foil paper.

Designs by Lauren Johnston

Child's Activity Tray

**Frolicking frogs add up to fantastic fun!
Our patterns make this an easy project.**

Materials

White paper
Masking tape
Bed tray
**Aleene's Premium-Coat™ Acrylic
    Paints: Medium Turquoise, True
    Turquoise, True Blue, True
    Green, Medium Green, White**
Waxed paper
2"-square kitchen sponge
Pop-up craft sponges
Felt-tip permanent black marker
Cotton swabs
Paintbrushes: liner, 1" sponge
Aleene's Enhancers™: Gloss Varnish

Directions

1 Tape paper to cover center of tray. Pour puddles of Medium Turquoise, True Turquoise, True Blue, and True Green onto waxed paper. Load kitchen sponge with True Turquoise and tap paint onto sides and edges of tray. Repeat with True Blue, True Green, and Medium Turquoise until entire tray frame is covered (see photo). Do not clean sponge between colors. Let dry. Remove paper from tray center.

2 Transfer patterns to pop-up sponge, using black marker. Cut out. Place each sponge into water to expand and wring out excess water. Referring to photo, sponge-paint frog bodies, legs, and footprints, using True Green. Let dry. Sponge-paint frog heads and feet, using Medium Green. Let dry. Dip cotton swab into Medium Green and paint toes on footprints. Dip another cotton swab into White and paint dots for eyes. Let dry. Paint child's name, using liner brush and True Blue. Let dry. Paint dots on ends of letters, using liner brush and True Turquoise. Let dry.

3 Add dots in eyes, lines in legs, front legs, dashed lines, lettering, and mouths, using marker (see photo). Dip cotton swab in True Blue and paint dots around edge of tray as desired. Let dry. Apply 1 coat varnish, using sponge brush. Let dry.

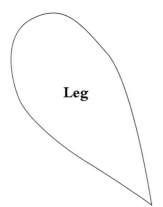

Leg

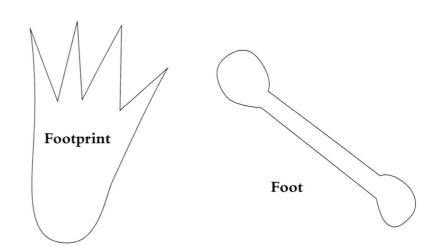

Footprint

Foot

Design by Cheryl Ball, SCD

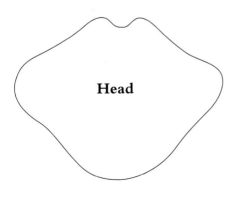

Head

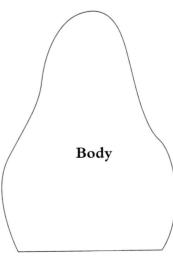

Body

Memories in Minutes

Designs by Joan Fee, SCD

Aleene's Botanical Preserved Flowers & Foliage makes instant pressed-flower jewelry a snap.

Materials
Iron
White paper
Aleene's Botanical Preserved Flowers and Foliage™
Cutting board
Aleene's Thick Designer Tacky Glue™
Tweezers
Desired jewelry
Small picture frame (optional)

Directions

Heat iron to medium, using dry setting. Fold paper in half and place flowers and foliage between paper. Place paper on cutting board and iron flowers. Press for approximately 10 seconds, turn paper over, and press for 10 seconds on other side. Let cool.

Cut desired pieces from pressed flowers and foliage. Dip ends of flowers or foliage into glue, using tweezers. Arrange on jewelry as desired. Let dry.

Using same technique, substitute small picture frame for jewelry and create a miniature picture for your home.

Back to School Tote

Let a tote-bag angel watch over your little ones as they go to and from school.

Materials
Tote bag
Cardboard covered with waxed paper to fit inside tote bag
Jeans pocket
Permanent black fabric marker
Aleene's Premium-Coat™ Acrylic Paints: Mustard Yellow, Light Pink, Brown, Medium Pink
Aleene's Enhancers™: Textile Medium
Waxed paper
Assorted paintbrushes
Thin cotton batting
Aleene's OK to Wash-It™ Glue
Plaid fabric scrap
7 (¼") snaps
Aleene's Jewel-It™ Glue
6" length jute
1⅓ yards ½"-wide burgundy rickrack
Brown kraft paper
Aleene's Paper Napkin Appliqué Glue™
Iridescent glitter dimensional paint

Directions

1 Wash and dry tote bag; do not use fabric softener in washer or dryer. Place cardboard covered with waxed paper inside tote bag.

2 Trace angel patterns (on page 74) onto jeans pocket, using marker; trace moon onto tote bag (see photo on page 75).

3 For each color of acrylic paint, mix equal parts paint and Textile Medium on waxed paper. Paint angel body and moon Mustard Yellow (see photo). Let dry. Paint face Light Pink. Let dry. Dab on Brown hair. Let dry. For cheeks, dab on Medium Pink.

4 Draw arms, legs, face, and detail lines of dress, using

Recycle a pocket from worn jeans for this tote bag.
(Photo of completed tote bag is on page 75.)

black marker. Add detail lines to moon (see photo at right).

5 Cut angel wings from batting. Glue to pocket, using OK to Wash-It. Let dry. Cut small heart from plaid fabric. Glue to angel, using OK to Wash-It Glue. Let dry.

6 Glue 3 snaps down front of dress, using Jewel-It Glue (see photos). Apply glue to back of each snap and press in place on angel body. Be sure to use enough glue so that glue comes up around sides of each. (Glue dries clear.)

7 Tie jute in bow and glue to top of angel's hair, using OK to Wash-It. Let dry. Glue pocket to tote bag, using OK to Wash-It. Let dry. Glue rickrack around edges of tote bag, using OK to Wash-It (see photo). Let dry. Glue 1 of remaining snaps in each corner of rickrack, using Jewel-It (see Step 6).

8 Draw stars on kraft paper and cut out. Brush Napkin Appliqué Glue onto tote bag where desired and press stars into glue. Brush more glue over stars. Let dry. Brush iridescent glitter around stars and over angel body (see photo). Let dry. Write desired message or name on tote bag, using black marker. Remove cardboard from inside tote bag.

9 Do not wash tote bag for at least 2 weeks. Turn tote bag wrong side out, wash by hand, and hang to dry.

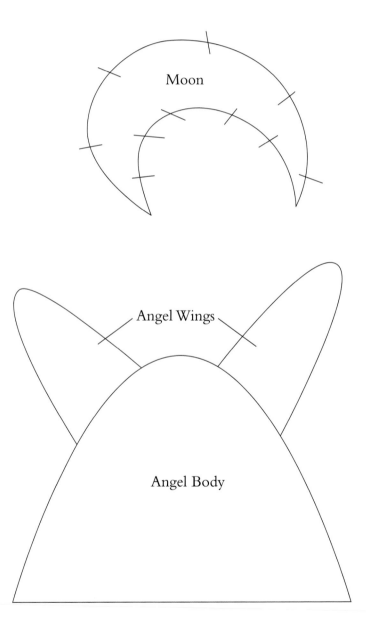

Moon

Angel Wings

Angel Body

Fashion

Use the simple techniques in this chapter to turn T-shirts, sweatshirts, and other purchased garments into wearable art.

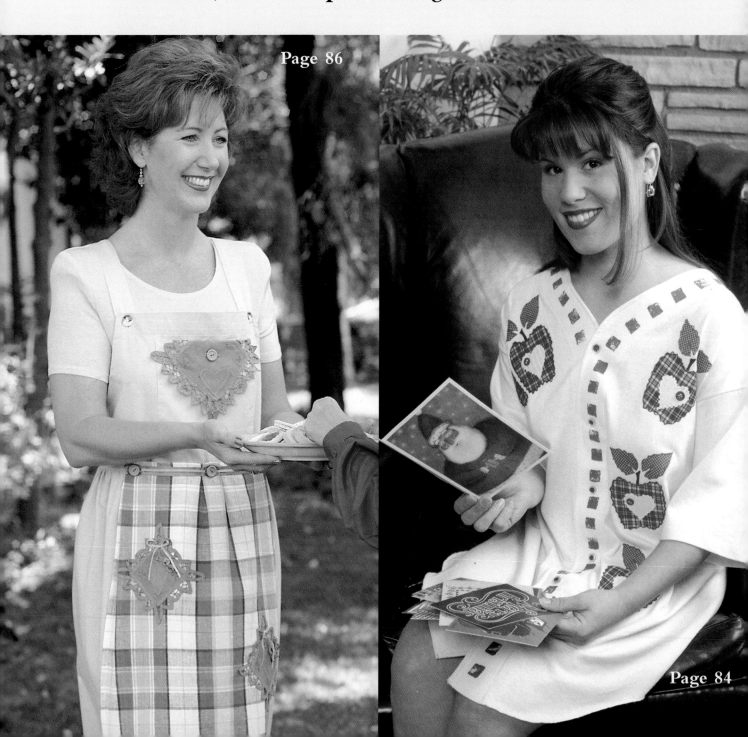

Page 86

Page 84

Magic

Autumn Colors

Here's an easy addition to your fall casual wardrobe. Fuse leaf shapes onto a shirt and then decorate with dimensional paints.

Materials
Long-sleeved T-shirt or sweatshirt
Fine-tip permanent black marker
Lightweight cardboard
Aleene's Fusible Web™
4 (8") squares fabric in various fall prints
Cardboard covered with waxed paper
Dimensional fabric paint pens: copper, silver
8 assorted buttons to match fabrics

Directions

Note: See page 5 for tips on working with fusible web.

1 Wash and dry shirt; do not use fabric softener in washer or dryer. Transfer patterns to cardboard and cut out.

2 Fuse web to wrong side of fabric squares. Trim 2 squares to 5" each. Center and trace 1 leaf on diagonal in each 5" square, using cardboard patterns (see photo). Cut leaf from center of each square; do not cut from outside edge. Then trace and cut out 2 leaves from remaining prints.

3 Referring to photo, fuse cutouts in place. Place cardboard covered with waxed paper inside shirt. Outline leaves and add details, using paint pens. Let dry. For each button, place small puddle of copper paint onto sweatshirt in desired position. Press button into paint so that paint comes up through holes in button. Let dry.

4 Do not wash shirt for at least 1 week. Turn shirt wrong side out, wash by hand, and hang to dry.

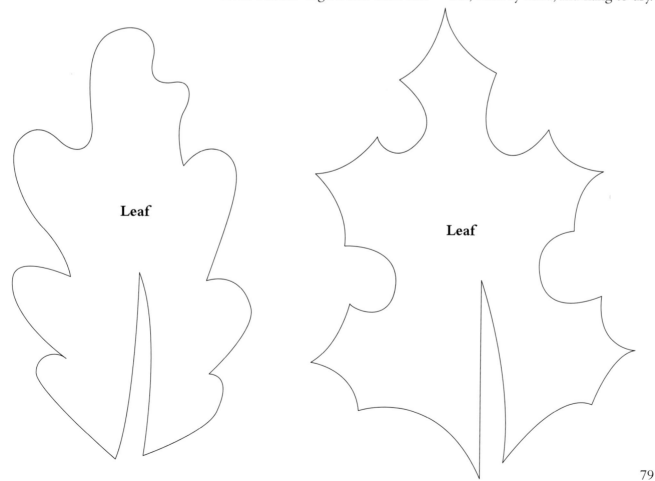

Leaf

Leaf

FaNcY FoiL JeWeLRY

**Even your jeweler won't be able to tell
that these baubles are really made of Shrink-It™.**

Materials
Aleene's Opake Shrink-It™ Plastic
Fine-grade sandpaper
Fine-tip permanent black marker
Aleene's Baking Board™ or non-stick cookie sheet, sprinkled with baby powder
Cotton gloves or fabric to protect hands
Spray paint: gold, silver, or copper
Aleene's 3-D Foiling Glue™
Aleene's Crafting Foil™: gold or silver
Aleene's Thick Designer Tacky Glue™
Jewelry findings: earring backs, pin backs

Directions

1 Sand 1 side of Shrink-It so that markings will adhere. Be sure to sand thoroughly both vertically and horizontally.

2 Using black marker, trace desired patterns onto sanded side of Shrink-It. (Marker ink may run on sanded surface; runs will shrink and disappear during baking.) Cut out designs, working just inside traced lines.

3 Preheat toaster oven or conventional oven to 275° to 300°. Place designs on room-temperature baking board and bake in oven. Edges should begin to curl within 25 seconds; if not, increase temperature slightly. If edges begin to curl as soon as designs are put in oven, reduce

heat. After about 1 minute, designs will lie flat. Wearing gloves or holding piece of fabric, remove designs 1 at a time from oven and immediately shape. Let cool. Spray-paint each design as desired. Let dry.

4 Apply 3-D Foiling Glue to each design as desired (see photos). Let dry. (Glue is sticky when dry. Glue must be thoroughly dry before foil is applied.) To apply foil, lay foil dull side down on top of glue lines. Using finger, press foil onto glue, completely covering glue with foil. Peel away foil paper.

5 If desired, glue dimensional design (see butterfly or star in photos) onto square base, using Tacky Glue. Glue jewelry finding to back of each design.

Heart

Base

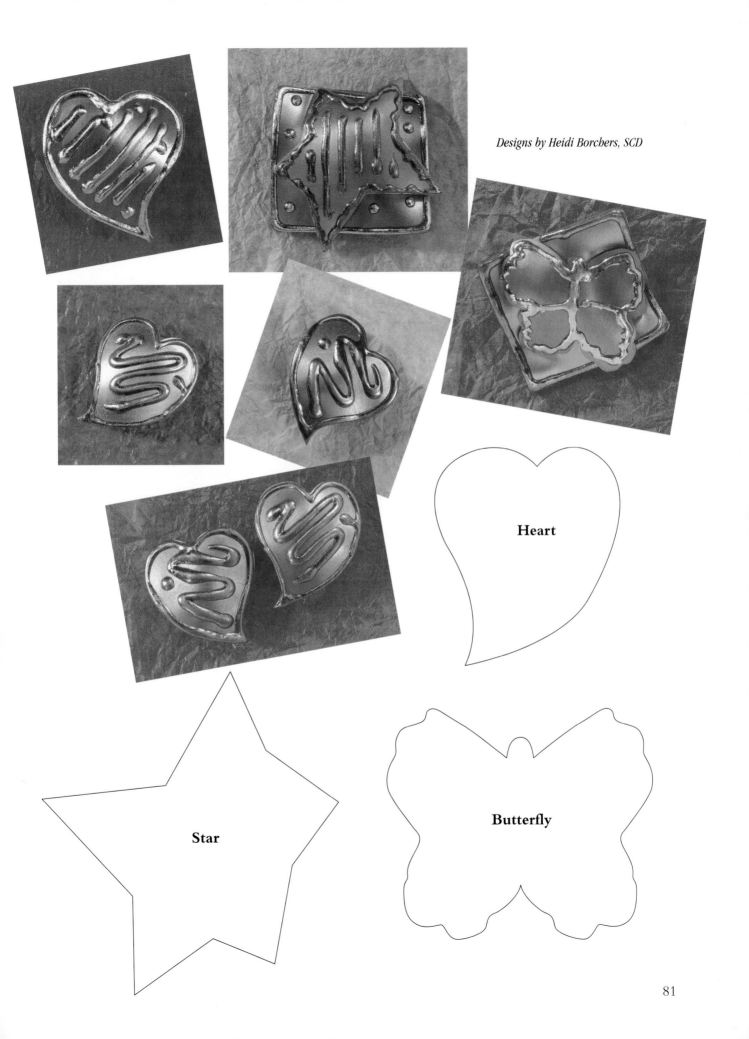

Designs by Heidi Borchers, SCD

Heart

Star

Butterfly

81

Tropical Temptations

Use cut-up fruit or craft sponges to stamp shapes onto fabric for a beach cover-up.

Materials
2 yards prewashed fabric (hemmed on all sides)
Iron
Aleene's Premium-Coat™ Acrylic Paints in desired colors
Aleene's Enhancers™: Textile Medium
Paper plate
Pop-up craft sponges (optional)
Citrus fruit, cut in half (optional)
Paper towels

Directions
Note: You can also use fabric as tablecloth. Or stamp prewashed canvas bag, canvas shoes, or other fabric items.

1 Wash and dry fabric; do not use fabric softener in washer or dryer. Iron out any wrinkles. Lay fabric, right side up, on covered work area.

2 Pour small puddle of each color of paint onto paper plate. For each, mix equal parts paint and Textile Medium. **For sponge-painted designs,** draw desired shapes on sponges and cut out. Place each sponge into water to expand and wring out excess water. Dip sponge into desired paint and blot excess paint on paper towel. Press sponge onto fabric where desired. Let dry. **For fruit-stamped designs,** dip cut side of fruit into paint and blot excess paint on paper towel. Press fruit half onto fabric where desired. Repeat as desired. Let dry.

3 To wear fabric as beach cover-up, wrap loosely around body and tie ends behind neck (see photo at left). Do not wash fabric for at least 1 week. Before first laundering, heat-set colors by ironing fabric from wrong side, using hottest setting recommended for fabric type. To launder, wash by hand and hang to dry.

Designs by Darsee Lett & Pattie Donham

Apple Shirt

Fuse apples and hearts to a jersey for your favorite teacher.

Materials

White baseball jersey
Aleene's Fusible Web™
Fabric scraps: burgundy plaid, green, white
Pop-up craft sponge
Acrylic paint to match green fabric scraps
Dimensional paints: dark green, brown, wine, white
Aleene's Enhancers™: Textile Medium
Waxed paper
Paper towels
Cardboard covered with waxed paper
4 (½") burgundy buttons

Directions

Note: See page 5 for tips on working with fusible web.

1 Wash and dry jersey; do not use fabric softener in washer or dryer. Transfer apple desired number of times to paper side of fusible web; also trace 2 leaves and 1 heart per apple. Cut out shapes roughly. Fuse apples to wrong side of burgundy plaid fabric, leaves to green fabric, and hearts to white fabric. Cut out shapes along marked lines. Fuse in place on jersey (see photo).

2 Cut 1" square from sponge. Place square into water to expand and wring out excess water. Pour small puddle of green acrylic paint onto waxed paper.

Mix equal parts paint and Textile Medium. Dip sponge into paint and blot excess on paper towel.

Lay jersey flat. Place cardboard covered with waxed paper inside jersey. Press sponge onto jersey to paint edging, letting front of jersey dry before continuing along back edge (see photo). Using dimensional paints, paint wavy line around each leaf with dark green; apple stems with brown; wavy line around each apple and dots on front buttons with wine; and edging around hearts and random dots on jersey with white. Let dry. To attach each button to heart, squeeze small puddle of white dimensional paint onto garment in desired position. Press button into dimensional paint so that paint comes up through holes in button. Let dry.

3 Do not wash jersey for at least 1 week. Turn garment wrong side out, wash by hand, and hang to dry.

Leaf

Apple

Heart

Design by Cheryl Ball, SCD

Dish Towel Apron

Doilies and a dish towel turn a plain jumper into a colorful garment.

Materials
Aleene's Fusible Web™
4" x 10" piece muslin
Aleene's Premium-Coat™ Acrylic
  Paints: Dusty Mauve, Dusty
  Beige, Dusty Green, Dusty Blue
Aleene's Enhancers™: Textile
  Medium
Paper plates
Paintbrushes: ½" flat, liner
Blue square doilies: 3 (3"), 1 (5")
Wooden buttons: 6 (½"), 4 (¾")
Sandpaper
Tack cloth
Plaid dish towel
Aleene's Tack-It Over & Over Glue™
Large-eyed needle
Pearl cotton: mauve, blue
Ribbons: 1 yard mauve satin,
  ½ yard grosgrain to match
  dish towel
Aleene's OK To Wash-It Fabric
  Glue™
Beige jumper with pocket on bib
Straight pins

Directions

Note: See page 5 for tips on working with fusible web.

1 Fuse web to wrong side of muslin. Lightly trace hearts onto muslin (see patterns below and on page 88).

2 Pour small puddle of each color of paint onto paper plate. For each, mix equal parts paint and Textile Medium. Paint each heart Dusty Mauve, using flat brush. Let dry.

3 **For Heart 1,** mix Dusty Mauve with Dusty Beige to lighten as desired. Paint center heart with mixture (see pattern). Let dry. Paint leaves Dusty Green, using liner brush and comma stroke. Let dry. Thin Dusty Beige with water to ink consistency and paint around edge of heart, using liner brush. Let dry. **For Heart 2,** paint rose in center, using Dusty Blue (see pattern). Let dry. Paint leaves Dusty Green, using liner brush and comma stroke. Let dry. Dab Dusty Mauve in center of rose. Thin Dusty Beige with water to ink consistency and paint stitching lines around outside edge of heart. Let dry. **For Hearts 3 and 4,** refer to patterns to paint designs, using liner brush and Dusty Beige. Let dry.

4 Cut out painted hearts. Fuse Heart 1 in 1 corner of large doily. Using flat brush, paint large buttons and 3 small buttons with Dusty Beige and remaining small buttons with Dusty Mauve. Let dry. Lightly sand edges to highlight. Wipe buttons with tack cloth to remove any dust.

5 Fuse web to wrong side of small doilies. Fuse small doilies to dish towel (see photo). Apply Tack-It Over & Over to edges of large doily. Let dry overnight.

6 To attach 2 small buttons to each heart on small doily (see photo), using pearl cotton and working from underneath, pull needle through each button and fabric, leaving long tail. Bring needle back through button to

Heart 1

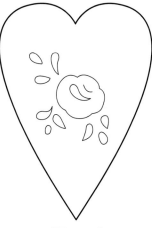

Heart 2

Change the look of your
Dish Towel Apron by using
different color doilies and
dish towel.

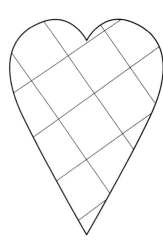

Heart 3

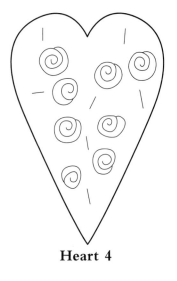

Heart 4

Design by Bonnie Stephens

wrong side of fabric and remove needle. Tie tails in square knot. Cut satin ribbon into 3 equal pieces. Tie each piece in bow. Glue 1 bow to each small doily, using OK To Wash-It (see photo). Let dry.

7 Pleat dish towel to fit jumper waistline. Pin grosgrain ribbon at top of dish towel to hold pleats in place (see photo). Stitch or fuse ribbon to waistband. Using 1 large button as guide, measure and mark 3 evenly spaced buttonholes on ribbon. Stitch buttonholes through ribbon and dish towel. Mark button placement on jumper waistband. Stitch 3 large buttons to jumper, using pearl cotton. Make 1 large buttonhole in large doily (see photo). Stitch remaining large button to center top of jumper pocket. Button dish towel to waistband of jumper. Position large doily on jumper bib and button it in place. Fold top edge of doily to inside of pocket.

88

Cat's Meow Pin

Design by Maria Nerius

Wear your love of cats on your collar with this posterboard pin.

Materials
Posterboard
Aleene's Enhancers™: All-Purpose Primer, Satin or Gloss Varnish
Aleene's Premium-Coat™ Acrylic Paints: Black, White, Light Fuchsia, Blush, Light Green, Light Blue
Paintbrushes: flat, fine liner
Paper towels
Toothpicks
Fine-tip permanent black marker
Aleene's Jewel-It™ Glue
1" pin back

Directions

1 Transfer cat head to poster-board 3 times. Cut out. Apply 1 coat of primer to 1 side of each head. Let dry. Paint 2 heads Black and 1 head White. Let dry.

2 Dip flat brush into White and blot on paper towel until you can barely see paint. Pounce brush on each black cat to paint face (see photo and patterns). Paint nose with Light Fuchsia on each black cat and with Black on white cat, using liner brush. Paint cheeks with Light Fuchsia on each black cat and with Blush on white cat, using flat brush and very little paint. Dot on eyes with Light Green on each black cat and with Light Blue on white cat, using toothpicks. Let dry. Outline white cat face with dotted line, using black marker. Draw whiskers and freckles on cat faces, using black marker (see photo and patterns). Add inner ear details to each black cat with White, using liner brush. Let dry. Apply 1 coat of varnish to each cat face. Let dry.

3 Apply Jewel-It Glue to back of white cat face. Press white cat face onto black cat faces to join (see photo). Let dry. Glue pin back to back of cats. Let dry.

Black Cat
(left in photo)

White Cat

Black Cat
(right in photo)

Watermelon Dresses

Brighten your wardrobe with whimsical watermelon wedges.

Materials

T-shirts: 1 each adult- and child-sized
Fabrics: 2 yards for adult, 18" x 45" piece for child
Aleene's Fusible Web™ (optional)
Straight pins
Cardboard sheets, each covered with waxed paper
Masking tape
Pop-up craft sponges
Fine-tip permanent black marker
Aleene's Premium-Coat™ Acrylic Paints: True Green, Holiday Green, True Red, Black
Aleene's Enhancers™: Textile Medium
Waxed paper
Paper towels
2" square kitchen sponge
Red buttons: 7 (½"), 1 (1")
Dimensional fabric paints: white, bright green

Directions

Note: If using fusible web, see page 5 for tips on working with fusible web.

1 Wash and dry T-shirts and fabrics; do not use fabric softener in washer or dryer.

2 Cut T-shirts straight across, 5" below armhole for adult and 2" below armhole for child. Cut fabric for adult shirt into 2 (1-yard) lengths and sew together along sides to form tube. Sew child's fabric together at selvages to form tube. Fold up ¼" double hem on each skirt and stitch or fuse in place.

3 For each skirt, run gathering stitches along top edge. Pull threads to gather top edge of skirt to fit bottom of corresponding T-shirt. Pin skirt in place on T-shirt and stitch.

4 Working on 1 dress at a time, place cardboard sheets covered with waxed paper inside T-shirt and under portion of skirt you plan to paint. Tape down areas to be painted to secure. Transfer patterns (on page 92) to sponges and cut out. Place each sponge into water to expand and wring out excess water. Pour small puddle of each color of paint onto waxed paper. For each, mix equal parts paint and Textile Medium. Referring to photo for color and positioning, dip sponge shape into paint and blot excess paint on paper towel; press sponge onto garment. Starting with wave sponge and True Green, first press wave at center front of shirt and then work up toward each shoulder, creating curve. Let dry. Using square sponge, paint Holiday Green at top of each wave. Let dry.

Design by Cheryl Ball, SCD

5 Using kitchen sponge and True Red, paint center of watermelon at neck of shirt, leaving white space between red and wavy green line (see photo). Let dry.

Pour puddles of True Green and Holiday Green next to each other on waxed paper. Dip leaf sponge into paints to cover sponge with darker green on lower edge of leaf. Press onto shirt (see photo). Repeat to sponge-paint second leaf. Let dry. Dip seed-shaped sponge into Black and press on shirt to paint seeds. Let dry. Referring to photo, repeat to paint designs on skirt.

6 Using dimensional paints, paint wavy lines at neck and in between red and green at neck, highlight seeds, and add random dots with white; paint wavy line in dark section of watermelon rind and add leaf veins and tendrils with green. Using large button on adult skirt, 1 small button on child's skirt, and 3 small buttons on each top, attach each button by squeezing small puddle of white dimensional paint above leaves. Press button into paint so that paint comes up through holes in button. Let dry.

7 Do not wash garments for at least 1 week. Turn garments wrong side out, wash by hand, and hang to dry.

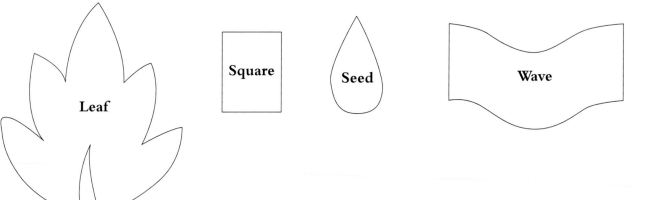

Leaf

Square

Seed

Wave

Smart'n'Sassy Vest

This crocheted vest looks great with everything from skirts to jeans.

Design by Carol Alexander

Materials

Caron Wintuk 4-ply worsted-weight yarn, 100-gram/3.5-ounce skeins: 4 (5, 6) mulberry
Crochet hook: size 5/F or 4-mm (6/G or 4.25-mm, 8/H or 5-mm) or size to obtain gauge
Yarn needle

Note: Materials and directions are given for size small, with information for sizes medium and large listed in parentheses.

Directions
Gauge
1 square motif = 3¾" (4⅛", 4½")

To make sure garment fits as desired, take time to check gauge.

Sizing Information

	S	M	L
Bust Measurement	34"	38"	42"
Finished Bust Measurement	38½"	42¼"	46"
Finished Length	18¾"	20⅝"	22½"

See page 22 for list of abbreviations and other general directions.

Special Stitches

Triple crochet cluster (cl): Holding back last lp of each st on hook, work 2 tr, yo, draw through all 3 lps on hook.

Picot: Ch 3, sl st in 3rd ch from hook.

4-ch picot: Ch 4, cl st in 4th ch from hook.

Shell (sh): Work (3 dc, ch 2, 3 dc) in next st.

Vest
Square Motif (Make 42.)

With size hook to obtain gauge, ch 6, sl st to first ch to close ring.

Rnd 1: Ch 4, tr in ring, ch 4 (cl, ch 4) 7 times in ring, sl st to top of beg ch-4: 8 petals.

Rnd 2: Ch 1; ★ sc in top of petal, (2 sc, picot, 2 sc) in next ch-4 sp, sc in top of next petal, ch 8, turn, sk last 5 sc worked, sl st in next sc (top of petal), ch 1, turn, work 16 sc in ch-8 sp just made, (2 sc, picot, 2 sc) in next ch-4 sp; rep from ★ around, sl st to beg ch-1.

Rnd 3: Ch 6 (counts as dc and ch 3), sk next 6 sc, sc in next 2 sc, ch 2, sc in next 2 sc, ch 3, ★ sk 5 sc, dc in last sc worked in ch-8 sp, ch 4 ★★, dc in base of next ch-8 sp, ch 3; rep from ★ around, ending last rep at ★★, sl st to 3rd ch of beg ch-6. Fasten off.

Triangle Motif (Make 2.)

Ch 6, sl st to first ch to close ring.

Rnd 1: Ch 8 (counts as tr and ch 4), (cl, ch 4) 3 times in ring, tr in ring; then working on straight edge of triangle, work 3 sc in side of tr, 2 sc in ring, 3 sc in beg ch-8 sp, sl st in 4th st of beg ch-8.

Rnd 2: Ch 1, sc in same st, (2 sc, picot, 2 sc) in first ch-4 sp, sc in top of next petal, ch 5, turn, tr in sc at beg of rnd, ch 1, turn, 8 sc in ch-5/tr sp, (2 sc, picot, 2 sc) in next ch-4 sp, (sc, picot, sc) in top of next petal, ch 8, turn, sk next sc and picot, sl st in next sc, ch 1, turn, 16 sc in ch-8 sp, [2 sc, picot, 2 sc] in next ch-4 sp, sc in top of next petal, rep bet [ ] once more, ch 8 (counts as tr and ch-5), turn, sl st in sc in top of last petal, ch 1, turn, 8 sc over next 5 ch, sl st in 6th ch, sc evenly along straight edge to beg of rnd; sl st to beg sc.

Rnd 3: Ch 1, (2 sc, ch 2, 2 sc) in same sc, ch 3, dc in sc in top of petal, ch 4, dc in base of next ch-8 sp, ch 3, sk 6 sc, sc in 2 sc, ch 2, sc in 2 sc, ch 3, sk 6 sc, dc in sc in top of next petal, ch 4, dc in base of next ch-8 sp, ch 3, (2 sc, ch 2, 2 sc) in last sc on this side, sl st in next sc. Fasten off.

Finishing
Joining Motifs

Beg at corner ch-2 sp, join 2 motifs on rs with sl st through all edge sts and chs from 1 corner to next. Fasten off. Foll Assembly Diagram, first join squares and triangles into strips where indicated and then join strips to complete vest. Sl st shoulder seams tog in same manner.

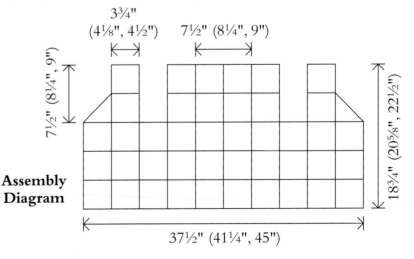

3¾"
(4⅛", 4½")   7½" (8¼", 9")

7½" (8¼", 9")

18¾" (20⅝", 22½")

Assembly Diagram

37½" (41¼", 45")

Armhole Edging

Rnd 1 (rs): Attach yarn at center underarm, ch 1, work sc evenly around armhole opening, sl st to beg sc.

Rnds 2 and 3: Rep Rnd 1 twice more, working any dec needed to keep work flat. Fasten off.

Body Edging

Rnd 1 (rs): Beg at lower edge, ch 1, work sc evenly around entire edge, working 3 sc at outer corners of lower fronts and at neck shaping, and dec in inner corner at neck as needed to keep garment flat; sl st to beg sc.

Rnds 2 and 3: Rep Rnd 1 twice more, adjusting with dec and inc as needed. Fasten off.

Lower Edging

Row 1 (rs): Holding vest upside down, attach yarn at right corner, ch 3 (counts as dc), 2 dc in same st; ★ sk 5 sts, sh; rep from ★ across, adjusting number of sk sts as needed, ending with sk 5 sts, 3 dc in last st at corner; turn.

Row 2: Ch 3 (counts as dc), 2 dc in same st; ★ ch 1, work sh in ch–2 sp at center of next sh; rep from ★ across, end ch 1, 3 dc in top of turning ch-3; turn.

Row 3: Work 4-ch picot, sc in first dc; ★ 3 dc in next ch-1 sp, (sc, 4-ch picot, sc) in ch-2 at center of next sh; rep from ★ across, end last rep with sc in top of turning ch-3, 4-ch picot, sl st in last sc made. Fasten off.

Row 4: Attach yarn at base of first picot made on Row 3, ch 5, sk picot; ★ (2 dc, 4-ch picot, 2 dc) in center dc of next 3-dc group, ch 2; rep from ★ across, end last rep with ch-5 instead of ch-2, sk picot, sl st in side of ch-3 at beg of Row 2. Fasten off.

Crochet individual motifs and then join them, using a slip stitch.

Flowered Slicker

If you like the look of this slicker, paint an umbrella to match.

Materials
Pop-up craft sponges
Fine-tip permanent black marker
Aleene's Premium-Coat™ Acrylic Paints: Medium Fuchsia, Holiday Red, True Orange, True Green, White
Aleene's Enhancers™: Textile Medium
Waxed paper
Paper towels
Child-sized yellow slicker
Cotton swabs
Dimensional fabric paints: pink, bright orange, green, bright yellow, white

Directions

1 Transfer patterns to sponges and cut out. Place each sponge into water to expand and wring out excess water.

2 Pour small puddle of each color of paint onto waxed paper. For each, mix equal parts paint and Textile Medium. Referring to photos for colors, dip sponge into paint and blot excess paint on paper towel. Press sponge onto slicker. Paint in following order, letting dry between colors: Medium Fuchsia, Holiday Red, True Orange, True Green, and White. Randomly paint dots, using cotton swabs and White.

3 Using dimensional paints, add wavy lines around flowers with pink and orange, veins in leaves with green, circles in flower centers with yellow, and wavy lines at top of pockets and on slicker placket with white. Let dry.

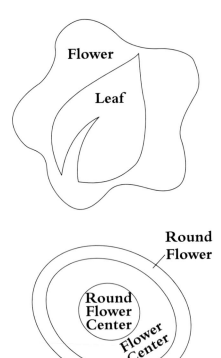

Flower

Leaf

Round Flower

Round Flower Center

Flower Center

Designs by Cheryl Ball, SCD

Incredible Shrinking Jewelry

This project is fast, fun, and easy enough for kids to make.

Materials

Aleene's Clear Shrink-It™ Plastic
Fine-grade sandpaper
Extra-fine-tip permanent black marker
Aleene's Baking Board™ or non-stick cookie sheet, sprinkled with baby powder
Aleene's Premium-Coat™ Acrylic Paints: Medium Fuchsia, True Red, True Yellow, True Green, True Violet, Medium Green, White
#4 round paintbrush
Aleene's Enhancers™: Gloss Varnish
Aleene's Thick Designer Tacky Glue™
2 earring backs
5 white pony beads
2 yards white or brightly colored rattail cording

Directions

1 Sand 1 side of Shrink-It so that markings will adhere. Be sure to sand thoroughly both vertically and horizontally.

2 Using black marker, trace patterns onto sanded side of Shrink-It. (Marker ink may run on sanded surface; runs will shrink and disappear during baking.) Cut out designs just inside traced lines.

3 Preheat toaster oven or conventional oven to 275° to 300°. Place designs on room-temperature baking board and bake in oven. Edges should begin to curl within 25 seconds; if not, increase temperature slightly. If edges begin to curl as soon as you put designs in oven, reduce heat. After about 1 minute, designs will lie flat. Remove designs from oven. Let cool.

4 Place each design wrong side up on corresponding pattern and trace details, using black marker. Referring to photo, apply 2 coats of desired paint to each design, trying to stay inside lines and letting dry between coats. Apply 1 coat of varnish to each design. Let dry.

5 For earrings, glue 1 earring back to wrong side of each earring. Let dry. For necklace, glue side of pony bead on wrong side of each flower and heart at top. Let dry. Thread cording through bead on 1 heart. Center heart on cording. Tie knot on each side of bead to secure. Measure and mark equal distance on each side of heart and tie knot at each mark. Thread 1 flower onto cording at side of each knot and tie another knot to secure. Repeat to add 2 more hearts. Tie ends of necklace in knot.

Flower Pattern

Flower Details
(Smaller than actual size)

Heart

Holiday

**Deck your halls for the holidays
with these festive designs.**

Page 110

Page 127

Page 138

Crafting

Satin Sheen Heart Hanger

This easy bow with hearts dresses up your door—or just says how much you care.

Materials

Aleene's Premium-Coat™ Acrylic Paints: Medium Fuchsia, Dark Fuchsia, True Red, True Violet, Light Violet, True Fuchsia, Light Fuchsia, White
Paintbrush
5 (4"-wide) wooden hearts
Pop-up craft sponge
Fine-tip permanent black marker
Waxed paper
Paper towels
Cotton swabs
Aleene's Enhancers™: Gloss Varnish
5 (¼") screw eyes
Aleene's Satin Sheen Twisted Ribbon™: red
Aleene's Thick Designer Tacky Glue™
3 (½") buttons

Directions

1 Using 1 color per heart, paint both sides of wooden hearts with Medium Fuchsia, Dark Fuchsia, True Red, True Violet, and Light Violet, letting 1 side dry before turning over. Let dry.

2 Transfer scallop and heart patterns to sponge and cut out. Draw ¾" square on sponge and cut out. Place each sponge into water to expand and wring out excess water. Pour small puddle of each color of paint onto waxed paper. Referring to photo and list below, paint details, letting 1 color paint dry before using another. To sponge-paint, dip sponge into paint and blot excess on paper towel; then press sponge onto heart. To paint dots, small hearts, and wavy lines, dip cotton swab into paint, blot excess on paper towel, and press swab onto heart.

Clockwise from top (see photo): **For Medium Fuchsia heart,** paint True Fuchsia hearts freehand. **For Dark Fuchsia heart,** use heart sponge and Light Fuchsia; add White dots. **For True Red heart,** use square sponge and Medium Fuchsia; add Dark Fuchsia dots at corners of squares. **For True Violet heart,** use scallop sponge and White for edging; add White dots. **For Light Violet heart,** paint True Violet wavy line around heart; add White dots in clusters of 3. Let each heart dry.

Apply 1 coat of varnish to both sides of each heart, letting dry before turning over.

3 Insert 1 screw eye into top of each heart. Untwist 3 yards of twisted ribbon. Cut 1 (1-yard) length and 5 (½"-wide) strips. Thread 1 strip through each screw eye. Holding ribbon strips for all hearts together, adjust lengths so that hearts are staggered (see photo). Knot ends together.

4 Make large bow with four long tails from remaining twisted ribbon (see photo). Glue bow onto ribbon strips just below knot. Glue buttons to cover knot. Let dry.

Scallop

Heart

Design by Cheryl Ball, SCD

103

Design by Heidi Borchers, SCD

Door Decor

Use this heartwarming decoration inside or out, since Aleene's Satin Sheen twisted ribbon is waterproof and won't fade.

Materials
19"-wide cardboard heart shape
Aleene's Satin Sheen Twisted
    Ribbon™: red, white
Aleene's Glue Gun™
Aleene's Glue Sticks™: all-purpose
Pinking shears

Directions

1 To cover cardboard heart, untwist red twisted ribbon and cut 3 (16") and 2 (13") lengths. If glue gun is dual temperature, set to low. Glue long edges of lengths together to form sheet of ribbon, with 13" lengths at top and bottom. Let dry. Using cardboard heart as pattern, transfer heart to back of ribbon sheet, adding 2" all around. Cut out. Center cardboard heart on ribbon heart. Fold excess ribbon to back of cardboard heart and glue in place. Let dry.

2 Untwist white twisted ribbon and cut into 13 (4") lengths. Curve 1 end of each length to form scallop, using pinking shears. With scallops extending beyond edge, glue lengths to back of heart, overlapping pieces slightly (see photo). Cut 72" length of white ribbon. Tie in loose bow; shape and notch ends (see photo). Glue to top of heart. Let dry.

3 Cut 1 (18") length each of untwisted red and white ribbon. Tear into $\frac{1}{8}$"- to $\frac{1}{4}$"-wide strips. Knot strips together 6" from 1 end. Glue knot inside center loop of bow (see photo). Let dry.

4 For small hearts, cut 9 (2"-wide) hearts from 10" length of untwisted red ribbon. Glue hearts on bow as desired. Let dry.

Heart

Bunny Wreath

Make fuzzy bunnies from quilt batting for this Easter wreath.

Materials

Fabrics: ½ yard for wreath, ⅛ yard coordinating for loops
14"-wide craft foam wreath
Aleene's Thick Designer Tacky Glue™
⅛ yard or 3" x 27" piece cotton quilt batting
Aleene's Fabric Stiffener™
½" flat paintbrush
Straight pins
Polyester fiberfill
Clothespins (optional)
White quilting thread
Black fabric paint or fine-tip permanent black fabric marker
6 craft eyes
Ribbons: 1⅓ yards each ⅛"- or ¼"-wide in 3 colors, 2" length ¼"-wide to match wreath fabric
Aleene's Fusible Web™
Rotary cutter, cutting mat, and ruler (wave or pinking blade optional)
4 to 6 floral picks with Easter designs

Directions

Note: See page 5 for tips on working with fusible web.

1 Cut 9 (1" x 45") strips of wreath fabric. Wrap strips around wreath to cover, gluing strip ends to wreath. Let dry.

2 Transfer pattern to batting and cut 12 bunny ears. Apply thick layer of fabric stiffener to 1 side of 6 ears. Then place 1 of remaining ear pieces on top of each fabric-stiffener ear and press together. Fold ears to shape; prop or pin to hold shape until stiffener has dried.

3 Cut 6 (3"-diameter) circles from batting for bunny heads. For each head, glue 2 circles together around edge, leaving 3" opening. Let dry. Lightly stuff with fiberfill. Apply glue to both sides of opening. Place straight edge of 2 ears ½" into opening. Press opening edges together. Use clothespins to hold edges together until glue has dried, if desired.

4 Cut 13½" length of quilting thread. Apply fabric stiffener and straighten thread. Let dry. Referring to photo, paint or draw face on each bunny head. Glue on eyes. Let dry. Cut stiffened thread into 9 (1½") lengths. Glue center of 3 pieces under each nose. Let dry.

5 Cut 4 (12") lengths of each color ribbon. Fuse web onto wrong side of coordinating fabric. Fuse coordinating fabric to remaining wreath fabric. Cut 24 (1" x 6") strips from fused fabric, using rotary cutter (with wave or pinking blade, if desired). Fold 1 strip in half and gather ends together. Repeat with second strip. Overlap gathered ends, with loops in opposite directions. Tie strips together, using 12" ribbon length. Repeat to make 12 folded-loop pairs.

6 Pin folded-loop pairs and bunny heads to wreath (see photo). Cut off long ends of floral picks and insert picks into wreath. Make hanger by folding 2" ribbon length into loop and gluing ends to top back of wreath.

Ear

Design by Hancock Fabrics

Satin Sheen Bunny

A flowerpot forms the bunny's body for this charming holiday decoration.

Materials

4½"-diameter clay pot
Aleene's Premium-Coat™ Acrylic
   Paints: White, Light Blue, Light
   Fuchsia
Paintbrush
Pop-up craft sponge
Waxed paper
Paper towels
Aleene's Enhancers™: Gloss
   Varnish
Aleene's Satin Sheen Twisted
   Ribbon™: white, light blue
Aleene's Thick Designer Tacky
   Glue™
3 (12"-long) white chenille stems
Clothespins
3"-diameter craft foam egg
Straight pins
Pom-poms: 2 white and
   1 pink ½"-diameter, 1 white
   1½"-diameter
2 wiggle eyes
½" buttons: 1 blue, 3 pink

Directions

1 Apply 2 coats of White to pot, letting dry between coats. Cut ½" square from craft sponge. Place sponge into water to expand and wring out excess water. Pour small puddle of Light Blue onto waxed paper. Dip sponge into paint and blot excess on paper towel. Press sponge onto rim of pot to paint squares (see photo). Let dry. Apply 1 coat of varnish to pot. Let dry.

2 Transfer pattern to untwisted white ribbon and cut 4 bunny ears. Spread glue on 1 side of 1 ear piece and press 1 chenille stem into glue from tip of ear to base. Place another ear piece on top and align edges, sandwiching chenille stem in between. Hold together with clothespins until dry. Repeat to make second ear. Pour small puddle of Light Fuchsia paint onto waxed paper. On 1 side of each ear, paint inside with light coat (see photo). Let dry.

3 To make head, cut 16" length from remaining untwisted white ribbon. Tear into ¾"-wide strips. Spread glue on middle section of each ribbon strip. Apply strips to egg, 1 at a time, overlapping slightly to cover, placing middle of each strip at top of egg, and smoothing down along sides. Use straight pins to hold strips in place, letting free ends hang from bottom of egg. Let dry.

4 Twist ends of ribbons together at bottom of head and push into drainage hole in bottom of clay pot. Spread glue under bottom edge of head and pull ribbons tight. Let dry. Cut chenille stems in ears to about 1" and dip each into glue. Insert chenille stems into head, referring to photo for placement. Bend ears as desired.

5 For face, glue ½" white pom-poms side by side to make cheeks (see photo). Let dry. For whiskers, cut remaining chenille stem in half. Curl ends of each piece around pencil. Twist halves together in middle. Dip center of whiskers into glue and press onto face above cheeks. Let dry. Glue pink pom-pom at center of whiskers for nose. Let dry. Glue eyes in place. Let dry.

6 Untwist 18" of light blue ribbon and cut 1"-wide strip. Tie strip in bow around bunny neck and then shape. Glue blue button at center of bow and pink buttons down center front of pot (see photo). Let dry. Glue 1½" white pom-pom to center back of pot for tail. Let dry.

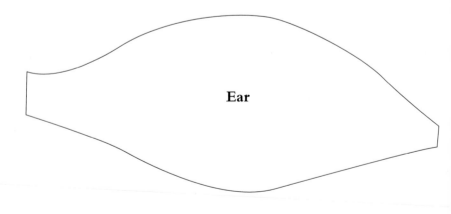

Ear

Design by Cheryl Ball, SCD

Patriotic Pots

For your Fourth of July picnic, these spirited pots hold flowers, citronella candles, or silverware.

Materials

For each: 1"-wide sponge
    paintbrush
Aleene's Premium-Coat™ Acrylic
    Paints: White, True Red, True
    Blue, Antique Gold
Clay pot in desired size
Pop-up craft sponge
Waxed paper
Paper towels
Aleene's Gloss Right-On Finish™

Directions

1 Using sponge brush, apply 2 coats of White to outside of pot, letting dry between coats. Wash brush thoroughly.

2 Transfer star patterns to pop-up sponge and cut out. Cut 1½" square from remaining pop-up sponge. Place each sponge into water to expand and wring out excess water.

3 **For horizontal-stripe pot,** pour puddles of True Red, True Blue, and Antique Gold onto waxed paper. Dip square sponge into True Red and blot excess paint on paper towel. Paint top of pot True Red (see photo). Let dry. Wash sponge thoroughly. Sponge-paint bottom of pot True Blue, leaving middle section White (see photo). Let dry. Using large star-shaped sponge and Antique Gold, sponge-paint stars on middle section of pot as desired. Let dry.

4 **For vertical-stripe pot,** pour puddles of True Blue, True Red, and Antique Gold onto waxed paper. Dip square sponge into True Blue and sponge-paint rim of pot. Let dry. Wash sponge thoroughly. Sponge-paint vertical stripes down sides of pot with True Red. Let dry. Using star-shaped sponges and Antique Gold, sponge-paint stars on pot as desired (see photo). Let dry.

5 **For each,** apply 1 coat of Right-On Finish to outside of pot. Let dry.

Stars

*Designs by
Ben Franklin Stores*

Patriotic Felt Flag

Don't worry if you don't have an outdoor location to post an American flag—you can still show patriotic pride by hanging this handsome felt banner on your front door.

Materials
72"-wide felt: ¾ yard red,
   1⅓ yards blue, ½ yard white,
   ¼ yard gold
Aleene's Fusible Web™
Straight pins
Embroidery needle
Black pearl cotton
Buttons: 2 each ¾" white and
   blue, 3 (¾") and 4 (1") red
25" length ½"-diameter wooden
   dowel
Aleene's Premium-Coat™ Acrylic
   Paint in shade to match blue felt
Sponge paintbrush
1 yard jute twine

Directions

1 From red felt, cut 1 (24" x 54") piece. From blue felt, cut 1 (24" x 54") piece, 1 (20" x 24") piece, and 4 (2" x 5") strips. Fuse web to 1 side of white felt, gold felt, and 20" x 24" blue felt piece. (You may need to piece fusible web.)

2 Referring to photo, transfer stripe pattern (on page 114) to white felt, repeating pattern as needed to make 3 (72"-long) stripes (see Diagram 1). Cut out.

Using patterns on page 114, transfer large star pattern 1 time and small star pattern 6 times to gold felt. Cut out.

3 Fuse 20" x 24" blue felt piece to 1 short end of red felt piece, aligning edges. Pin stripes in place on red felt piece (see photo). Once satisfied with positioning, trim edges of stripes as necessary. Remove pins and fuse stripes in place. Fuse large star on banner so that half of star is on blue area and half is on striped area (see photo). Fuse small stars in circle around large star.

4 Blanket-stitch along stripes and sew large hash marks on stars, using pearl cotton (see photo). Sew 1 (¾") small button where desired on each star.

5 With wrong sides facing and edges aligned, stitch banner front and 24" x 54" blue felt piece together, using ½" seam allowance. For hanging tabs, fold 2" x 5" blue felt strips in half and pin to top edge of banner, spacing evenly. Sew 1 (1") red button to center front of each tab, catching back of banner in stitching (see Diagram 2).

6 Paint dowel blue. Let dry. Slide dowel through hanging tabs. For hanger, tie 1 end of jute twine to each end of dowel.

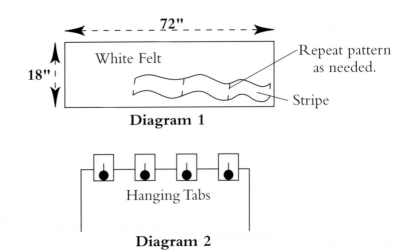

Diagram 1

Diagram 2

Design by Debi Schmitz

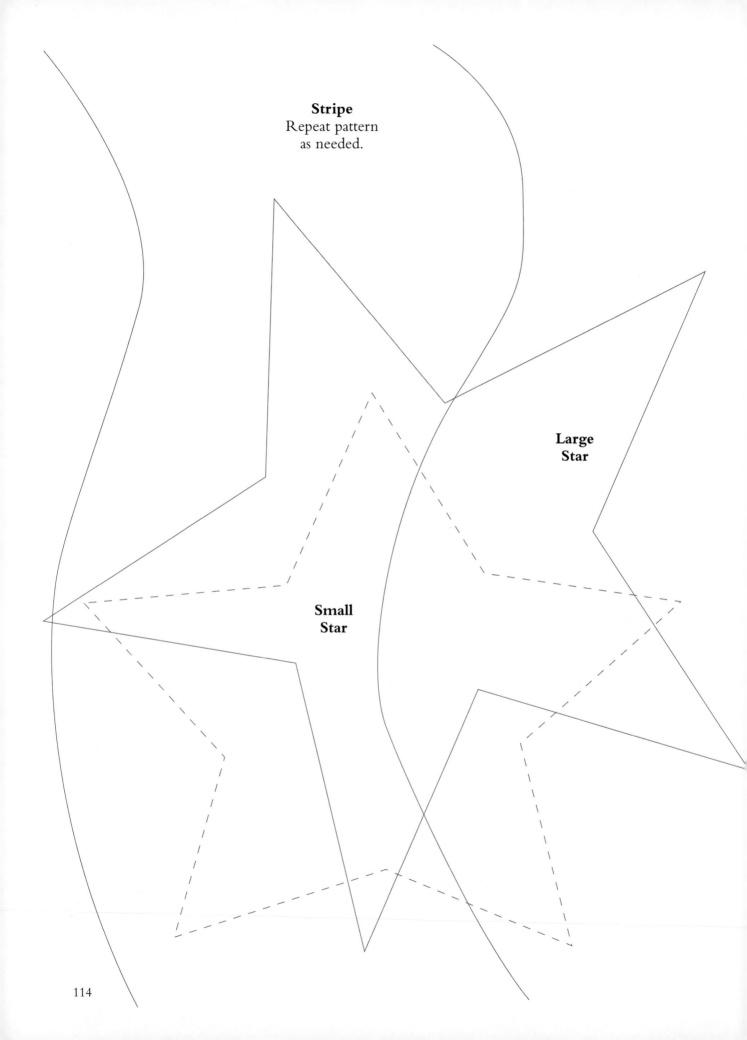

Stripe
Repeat pattern
as needed.

**Large
Star**

**Small
Star**

Fishbowl Pumpkins

Serve party snacks or trick-or-treat goodies from these painted containers. Few people will ever guess that the bases for these friendly faces are fishbowls!

Design by Cheryl Ball, SCD

Materials

For each pumpkin: **Thick kitchen sponge**

Aleene's Premium-Coat™ Acrylic Paints: True Orange, True Poppy, White, True Lavender, Black, True Yellow, Medium Orange

Aleene's Enhancers™: All-Purpose Primer, Gloss Varnish

Paper plates

Paper towels

Fishbowl

Pop-up craft sponge

Paintbrushes: ½" flat, round with stiff bristles, sponge

Cotton swabs

Fine-tip permanent black marker

Green raffia (optional)

Pinking shears (optional)

Yellow or purple fabric (optional)

Silk ivy leaves (optional)

Aleene's Thick Designer Tacky Glue™ (optional)

For lights shown in photo on page 117: **Craft knife**

20 black paper cups

¼"-diameter hole punch

Strand of 20 lights: orange or clear minilights

Directions

1 **For each pumpkin,** cut 1½" square from kitchen sponge. Mix 3 parts True Orange with 1 part primer on paper plate. Drizzle True Poppy over True Orange paint puddle. Do not mix. Dip sponge into paints, making sure to get both colors on sponge. Blot excess paint on paper towel. Sponge-paint outside of fishbowl. Let dry.

2 **For straight-stripe pumpkin,** cut 1" x 1½" piece from pop-up sponge. Place sponge into water to expand and wring out excess water. Pour puddle of True Poppy onto another paper plate. Dip sponge into True Poppy and blot excess on paper towel. Sponge-paint stripes down sides of fishbowl (see photo). Let dry.

For wavy-stripe pumpkin, use flat brush and True Poppy to paint wavy lines down sides of fishbowl (see photo). Let dry.

3 Transfer desired face patterns to pop-up sponge and cut out. Place sponge shapes into water to expand and wring out excess

water. Pour separate puddles of White, True Lavender, Black, and True Yellow onto paper plate. Sponge-paint eyes, nose, teeth, and mouth (see photo). Let dry. Use cotton swabs and True Lavender or White to paint dot on center of each eye. Dip end of bristles of dry round paintbrush into Medium Orange and pounce on cheeks. Let dry.

4 Use black marker to draw details (see photo). Using sponge brush, apply 1 coat of varnish to entire painted surface of fishbowl. Let dry.

5 If desired, tie raffia around top of bowl; or use pinking shears to cut strips of fabric and tie strips around top of bowl. If desired, glue silk ivy leaves to top of bowl. Let dry.

6 **For 1 strand of lights,** using craft knife, cut X in bottom of each cup. Use hole punch to punch holes around rim of each cup. Referring to photo and working from outside of cup, push 1 lightbulb on strand through X in bottom of each cup.

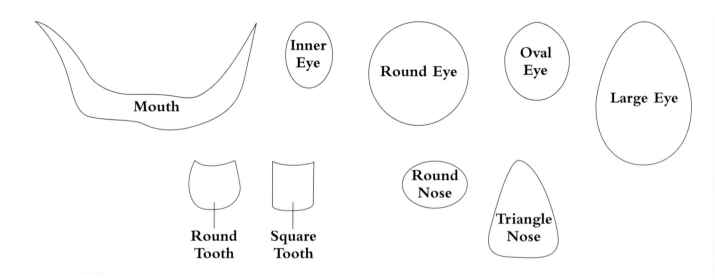

Mouth · Inner Eye · Round Eye · Oval Eye · Large Eye · Round Tooth · Square Tooth · Round Nose · Triangle Nose

design by Darsee Lett
d Pattie Donham

Cupcake *decorations*

These cheerfully frightful cupcake toppers double as Halloween jewelry. Tack-It Over & Over Glue™ makes it possible.

Materials

Aleene's Opake Shrink-It™ Plastic
Fine-grade sandpaper
Fine-tip permanent black marker
Colored pencils
Aleene's Baking Board™ or non-stick cookie sheet, sprinkled with baby power
Glitter dimensional paint
Aleene's Tack-It Over & Over Glue™

Directions

1 Sand 1 side of Shrink-It so that markings will adhere. Be sure to sand thoroughly both vertically and horizontally. Using black marker, trace desired patterns (on page 120) onto sanded side of Shrink-It. (Marker ink may run on sanded surface; runs will shrink and disappear during baking.) Referring to photo, use colored pencils to color each design. (Remember that colors will be more intense after shrinking.) Cut out designs. For each, cut 1 (1" x 6") stick of Shrink-It.

2 Preheat toaster oven or conventional oven to 275° to 300°. Place designs and sticks on room-temperature Baking Board and bake in oven. Edges should begin to curl within 25 seconds; if not, increase temperature slightly. If edges begin to curl as soon as designs are put in oven, reduce temperature. After about 1 minute, designs will lie flat. Remove designs from oven. Let cool.

3 **For bat,** use dimensional glitter paint to dot on eyes. Let dry. **For each design,** apply small amount of Tack-It Over & Over Glue to center back. Let glue dry for 12 to 24 hours. Place 1 Shrink-It stick onto glued area; insert stick into cupcake. To use decoration as jewelry, remove stick and press to clothing as desired.

Designs by Joan Fee, SCD

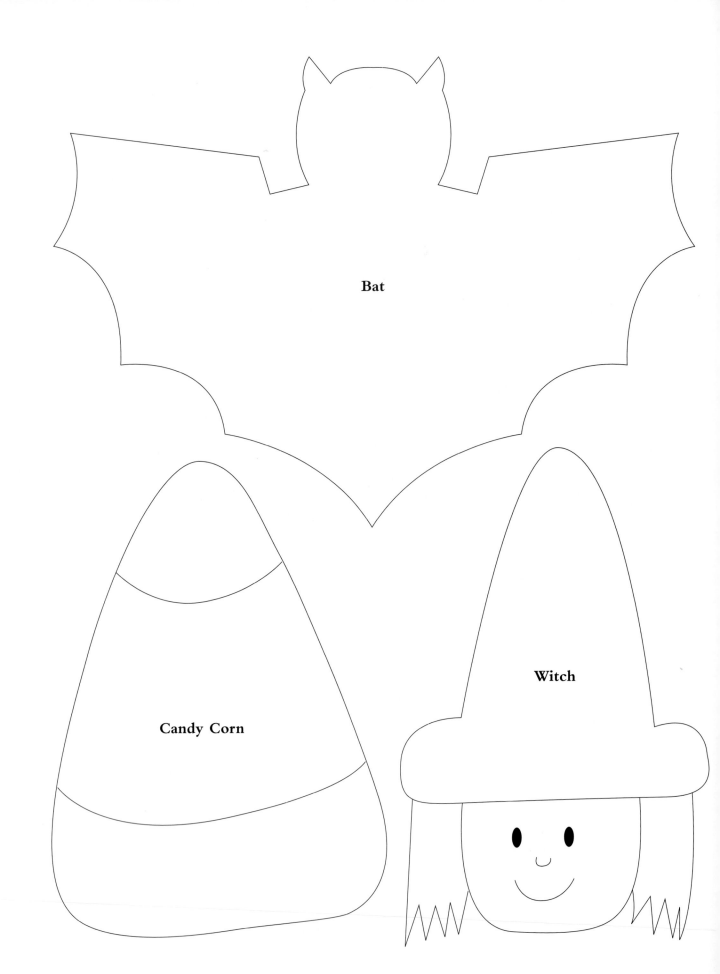

Bat

Candy Corn

Witch

Faux Gilded Ornaments

Add a rich look to your Christmas tree with simple tissue paper and foil.

Materials
Aleene's Tissue Paper™ in variety of colors
2"- to 3"-diameter glass ball ornaments
Spray paint in light color (optional)
Aleene's Paper Napkin Appliqué Glue™
½" shader paintbrush
Sea sponge
Aleene's 3-D Foiling Glue™
Aleene's Crafting Foil™: gold, silver
Decorative cording
Ribbon

Directions

1 **For each,** cut 2 to 3 (2" x 10") strips of tissue paper. Remove metal top and hanger from ornament. If desired, spray-paint ornament with light color and let dry.

2 Crumple each tissue strip and then flatten it, leaving some wrinkles. Working with 1 tissue strip at a time, apply Napkin Appliqué Glue to back of strip, ½" at a time, using brush. Wrap strip around ball, beginning at open end of ornament. Continue applying glue and wrapping strips around ball until ornament is covered, ending on opposite side from opening. Let dry. If you have small areas not covered by tissue paper, cut small pieces and glue to cover. Let dry.

3 Randomly sponge 3-D Foiling Glue around entire ball. Let dry overnight. To apply foil, lay foil dull side down on top of glue lines. Using finger, press foil onto glue, completely covering glue with foil. Peel away foil paper.

4 Replace metal top and hanger. Tie decorative cording to hanger. Tie ribbon in bow around top of ornament.

Design by Lauren Johnston

Snowman Angel Garland

Mix and match the textures of batting, felt, twine, and doilies for a beguiling garland of mittens, snowballs, and winged snowmen. Yes, Virginia, snowmen can be angels.

Materials

Cotton batting
Pearl cotton: red, navy, gold, green, brown, white
Embroidery needle
Polyester stuffing
Toothpicks
Aleene's Premium-Coat™ Acrylic Paint: True Orange
Small paintbrush
Aleene's Tacky Glue™
3 (8"-diameter) crocheted doilies
7 (4") paper Battenberg doilies, round or square
Assorted buttons
Felt scraps: red, gold, green
Fabric scraps in holiday colors
Twigs
1 (5") square each rib knit trim: red, navy, green
Gold jingle bells in assorted sizes
Small sponge
Strong coffee
12 (3"-diameter) craft foam balls
12 floral pins
2 yards jute
18-gauge floral wire
Glitter or glitter spray in desired color (optional)

Directions

1 **For each snowman,** transfer snowman pattern (on page 124) to batting and cut 2. Whip-stitch around edge, using desired color of pearl cotton and leaving 2" opening on 1 side for stuffing. Stuff snowman and then whipstitch opening closed. Stitch mouth and eyes, using brown pearl cotton. Paint 1 end of 1 toothpick True Orange. Let dry. Cut to desired length. Glue in place for nose.

2 For wings, gather 1 crocheted doily in center and tie to secure, using white pearl cotton. Glue or stitch gathered doily to back of snowman. Let dry.

Decorate snowman as desired with buttons and pieces of paper doily, felt, and fabric (see photo). For arms, glue twigs in place. Let dry.

3 For hat, fold and stitch long edges of desired color rib knit together. Fold up end for brim (see photo). Glue hat in place. Let dry. Tie top of hat with desired

Design by JO-ANN Fabrics & Crafts

color pearl cotton and tie on jingle bell (see photo). For antique look, dip sponge into coffee and dab onto snowman. Let dry.

4 **For each snowball,** cut strips of cotton batting and cover foam ball, gluing ends to secure. Let dry. Cut paper doily into pieces and glue onto ball as desired (see photo). Let dry. For hanger, glue floral pin in place, leaving ¼" exposed above surface of ball. Let dry. For antique look, dab with sponge dipped into coffee. Let dry.

5 **For each mitten,** transfer mitten pattern and cut 2 from felt and 1 from batting. Layer pieces, with batting in middle and edges aligned. Whipstitch together, leaving top open. Stuff lightly. Cut heart shape from desired color of felt. Glue paper doily pieces and felt heart in place (see photo). Let dry. Tie jingle bell to top corner over thumb (see photo). Repeat to make another mitten. Cut desired length of jute. Glue 1 end of jute into top of each mitten; glue top of each mitten closed. Let dry. For antique look, dab mittens with sponge dipped into coffee. Let dry.

6 To assemble garland, string pieces on floral wire (see photo). Twist, bend, and curl wire as desired. Sprinkle with glitter or spray with glitter spray, if desired.

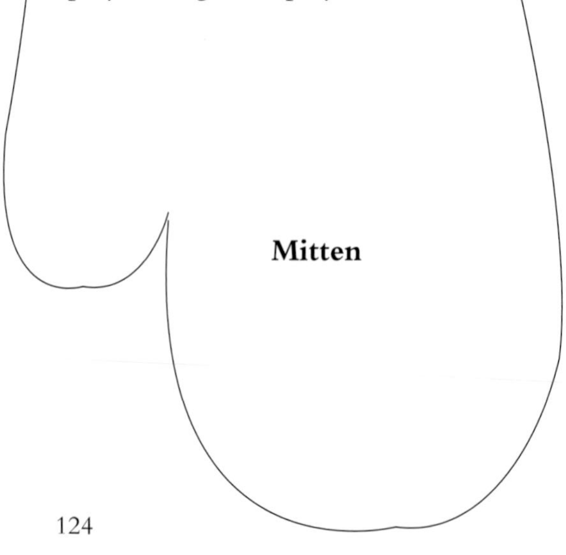

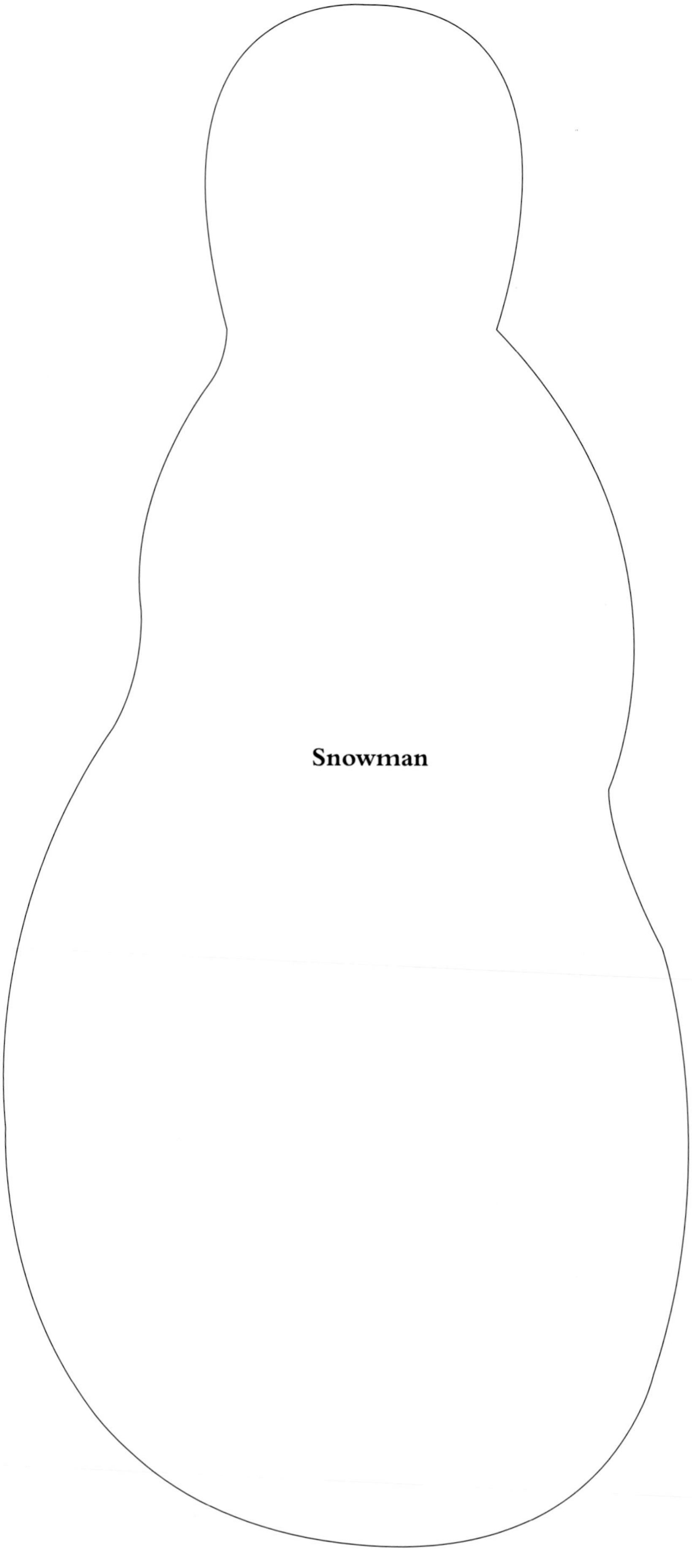

Snowman

Mitten

Treasure Tins

In festive red and green, these boxes make colorful holiday decorations. You could also make them in colors to match your bathroom or bedroom decor.

Materials

For each: **Round metal cookie tin with lid**
Delta Renaissance Foil Holiday Colors Kit
Delta Renaissance Foil Gold Crackle Kit
Sponge paintbrush
Desired lace and ribbons
Jingle bells (optional)
Botanical embellishments, such as gold holly leaves, pine sprigs, pinecones, gold and red berry sprays, dried flowers
Aleene's Tacky Glue™
26-gauge florist's wire (optional)

Directions

Note: Before beginning, please read and follow all directions included with Renaissance Foil Holiday Colors Kit and Renaissance Foil Gold Crackle Kit.

1 Apply Foil Sealer to cookie tin. Let dry. Apply Foil Adhesive to areas of tin that you plan to cover with lace. Let dry until adhesive is clear. Apply lace to adhesive-covered areas of tin, pressing lace down with your fingers to make sure it sticks to adhesive.

2 Paint tin with Foil Basecoat. **For red tins,** use red base coat. **For green tin,** use green base coat. **For gold tin,** use red base coat. Let dry.

Apply Foil Adhesive to all areas of tin that you wish to cover with foil. Let dry until adhesive is clear. Apply foil to all coated areas. To apply foil, lay foil dull side down on top of adhesive. Using finger, press foil onto glue, completely covering glue with foil. Peel away foil paper. Apply Foil Sealer to tin. Let dry.

3 **For gold box and lid of large red box,** use Foil Gold Crackle Kit. Follow directions on back of kit to apply Gold Foil to tin and lid. Brush on Foil Crackle Medium. Let crackle. Apply final coat of Foil Sealer. Let dry.

4 Trim as desired, referring to photo for inspiration. **For large red tin,** wrap fancy ribbon around tin and tie in bow. **For gold tin,** tie jingle bells and gold holly leaves to lid, using red cord. **For green tin,** make 1 (5-looped) bow with 1 tail and 1 (4-looped) bow with 2 tails; tie each bow center with length of floral wire. Glue 4-looped bow to tin lid and 5-looped bow on top of 4-looped bow. Let dry. Glue pine sprigs and pinecones around and under bows. Let dry. Glue gold holly leaves and gold berry sprays into bow. Let dry. **For small red tin,** make 2 bows as for green tin and glue to box lid. Let dry. Glue pine sprigs, pinecones, red berry sprays, and dried flowers around and inside bows. Let dry.

Designs by Joyce Bennett

Floral Ornaments

With a few dried flowers and some rich cording, transform inexpensive glass Christmas balls into elegant ornaments similar to those found in upscale boutiques.

Materials

For each: Clear or frosted glass ball ornament

Aleene's Thick Designer Tacky Glue™

Aleene's Botanical Preserved Flowers & Foliage™: ferns, variety of small flowers

Wire-edged ribbon (optional)

6" length satin cording

Directions for 1 ornament

1 Remove hanger cap from ornament. Apply thick bead of glue around top edge of ornament. Replace hanger cap. Let dry. (Glue allows hanger to support weight of decorated ornament.) Cut several 2" lengths of fern. Referring to photo, glue fern lengths to ornament. Let dry.

2 Beginning with flower pieces approximately 1" long, glue flowers in layers around top of ornament, cutting each successive layer of flowers shorter as you near top of ornament. If desired, tie length of wire-edged ribbon in bow, glue bow to top of ornament, and glue dried flowers around ribbon; let dry. Thread cording through hanger and knot ends.

Designs by Lauren Johnston

Tiny Table Tree

Buttons, jingle bells, chenille stems, and tiny bows make this Satin Sheen tree a merry addition to your holiday look. Use a larger cone to make a centerpiece tree.

Materials

Aleene's Satin Sheen Twisted Ribbon™: green
Aleene's Thick Designer Tacky Glue™
Wooden craft stick
10"-tall craft foam cone
Sequin pins
Rubber band
Candy cane chenille stems (or red and white chenille stems twisted together)
White kitchen string
Wooden stars: 1 (1½"), 12 (¾")
Aleene's Premium-Coat™ Acrylic Paint: True Yellow
½"-wide paintbrush
Toothpick
15 (½"-diameter) red or gold jingle bells
Straight pins
20 assorted buttons

Directions

1 Untwist 2 yards of green twisted ribbon. Cut 12 (3") lengths. Fold each piece in quarters lengthwise and cut curve on 1 end (see Diagram); unfold. Cut 3"-diameter circle from remaining green ribbon.

2 Apply line of glue to cone 2" from bottom edge, using craft stick. Slightly gather straight edge of each ribbon piece and press into glue, with curved edge at bottom (see photo). Secure with sequin pins every ½". Continue around cone, overlapping curved edges slightly, to within 1½" of top of tree. Apply glue to uncovered area of cone. Drape twisted ribbon circle over top of tree and hold in place until glue dries, using rubber band.

3 Cut chenille stems into 1½" lengths. Bend each into candy cane shape. Tie 12 small bows, using string. Paint stars and toothpick True Yellow. Let dry. Glue toothpick to 1 side of large star (see photo). Let dry.

4 Referring to photo, decorate tree. To position each jingle bell, poke straight pin into tree at angle, dip 1 bell into glue, and hang bell on pin. Let dry. Glue on small stars, buttons, chenille candy canes, and bows. Let dry. To place large star, dip end of toothpick into glue and stick into top of tree. Let dry.

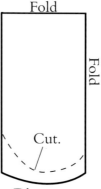

Fold

Fold

Cut.

Diagram

Nativity Miniquilts

Use these small fabric squares to decorate packages, wreaths, or Christmas trees—or string them together to make a garland. Because they're fused, they're fast to make.

Materials
Aleene's Fusible Web™
Fabrics: ½ yard solid for fronts,
   ¼ yard plaid for backing,
   scraps for appliqués
¼ yard fleece
Rotary cutter, mat, and ruler
   (optional)
Aleene's OK To Wash-It Glue™
Fine-tip permanent black fabric
   marker

Directions
Note: See page 5 for tips on working with fusible web.

1 Cut 5 (4") squares each from fusible web and fabric for fronts, 5 (6") squares each from fusible web and fabric for backing, and 5 (4¾") squares from fleece. Fuse web squares to wrong side of corresponding fabric squares. Center and fuse fronts on fleece squares.

2 Center front squares on wrong side of backing squares. Starting with 2 opposite sides, fold extended edges of backing to front and fuse in place. Repeat with remaining edges. Glue corners down, using 1 drop of glue per corner. Let dry.

3 Transfer appliqué patterns (on pages 130 and 131) to fusible web, using black marker. Roughly cut out patterns and fuse to fabric scraps as desired. Cut out along marked lines. Referring to photos, position appliqué pieces on miniquilt blocks. (Appliqué pieces can extend into borders.) Draw dashed lines around each appliqué piece, using fabric pen.

Design by Hancock Fabrics

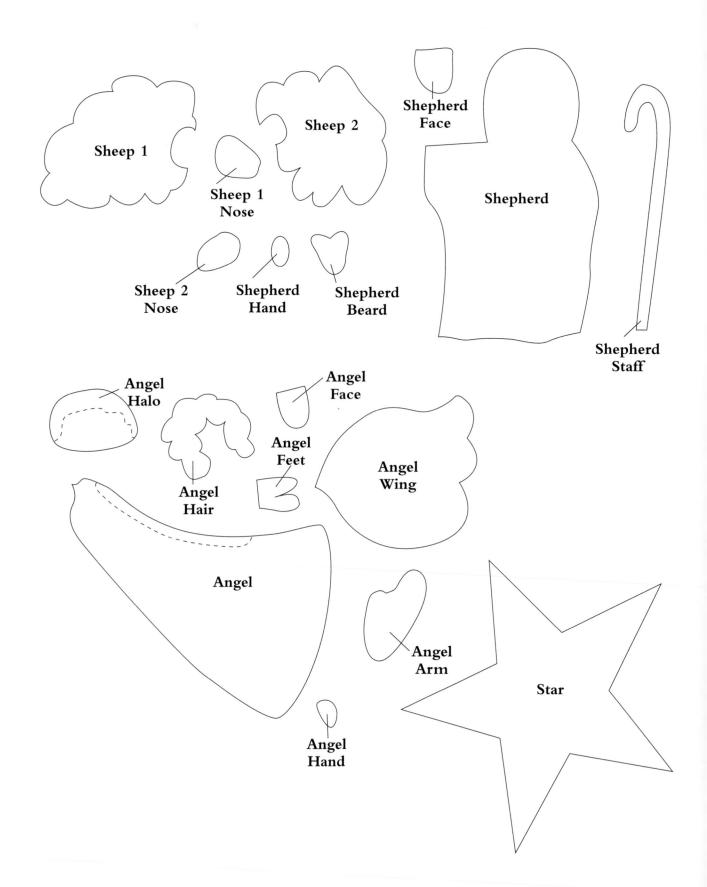

Sheep 1

Sheep 2

Shepherd
Face

Shepherd

Sheep 1
Nose

Sheep 2
Nose

Shepherd
Hand

Shepherd
Beard

Shepherd
Staff

Angel Halo

Angel
Face

Angel
Feet

Angel
Hair

Angel Wing

Angel

Angel
Arm

Star

Angel
Hand

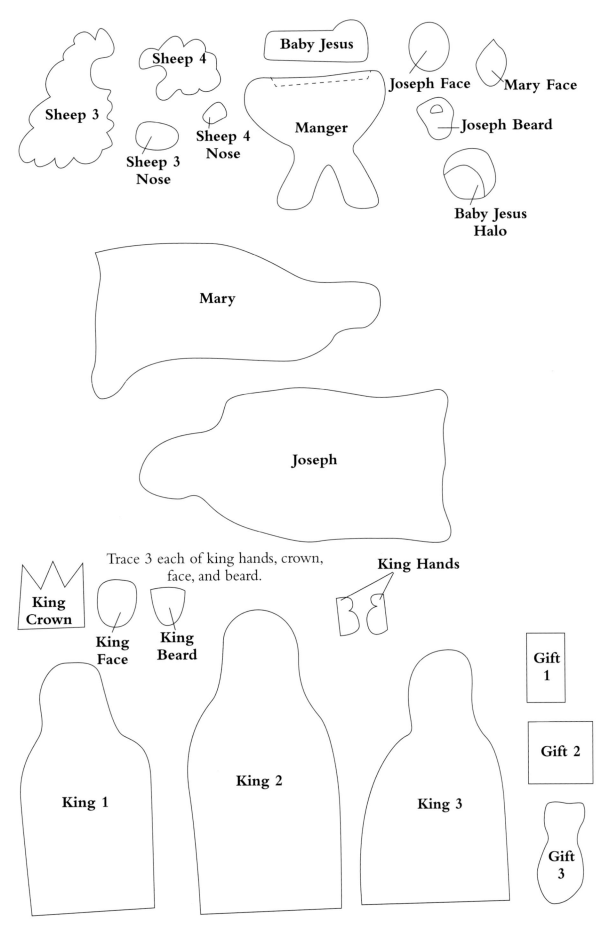

Sheep 4

Sheep 3

Sheep 3
Nose

Sheep 4
Nose

Baby Jesus

Manger

Joseph Face

Mary Face

Joseph Beard

Baby Jesus
Halo

Mary

Joseph

Trace 3 each of king hands, crown,
face, and beard.

King Hands

King
Crown

King
Face

King
Beard

Gift
1

Gift 2

King 1

King 2

King 3

Gift
3

131

Golden Cheesecloth Angel

Metallic spray paint gilds this simple angel. She takes her shape from an empty bottle.

Materials
4²⁄₃ yards cheesecloth
Plastic wrap
Aleene's Fabric Stiffener™
Zip-top plastic bag
2½"-diameter craft foam ball
Aleene's Tacky Glue™
11½"- to 13½"-tall glass or plastic bottle with long neck and wide base
4 white chenille stems
4 rubber bands
Fabric marking pen
1 package curly hair
Gold metallic spray paint (optional)
Straight pins
1¼ yards 1"- to 2"-wide wire-edged ribbon
18" length ¼"-wide ribbon
7" length narrow gold trim

Directions

1 Cut cheesecloth into 1 (45") square, 1 (54") square, and 2 (12½") squares. Cover flat work surface with plastic wrap. Pour 5 ounces of fabric stiffener and 2 capfuls of water into zip-top bag. Unfold all pieces of cheesecloth once, leaving 2 layers. Place 45" cheesecloth square into bag and thoroughly saturate with fabric stiffener. Place hand around opening of bag and, starting at 1 end of cheesecloth, pull cheesecloth out of bag, squeezing out excess fabric stiffener.

2 Place center of cheesecloth over top of bottle. Position cheesecloth evenly over 2 opposite sides of bottle and smooth out wrinkles. Puddle cheesecloth at base of bottle (see photo). Trim length, if desired.

3 Glue foam ball on top of bottle. To form arms, twist 3 chenille stems together, forming 1 thick stem. Push 1 end of chenille stem into each side of ball. Shape arms as shown in Diagram.

4 Refill zip-top bag with 5 ounces of fabric stiffener and 2 capfuls of water. Saturate 54" cheesecloth square with stiffener and remove from bag as in Step 1. Place center of cheesecloth over ball and smooth out wrinkles. Wrap 1 rubber band directly below ball and another rubber band below arms. Pull outer layer of cheesecloth up, blousing it around arms to form sleeves (see photo). Smooth out skirt, overlapping edges of previous piece. Puddle cheesecloth at base of bottle. Let dry.

5 Slide desired wing pattern (on page 134) under plastic wrap. Use large wing pattern for 13½" bottle or small wing pattern for 11½" bottle. Place remaining pieces of cheesecloth into bag with remaining fabric stiffener and saturate thoroughly. Working with 1 piece at a time, remove from bag as before. Stack saturated pieces smoothly on top of wing pattern. Pinch center until cheesecloth is inside pattern lines. Smooth out remaining cheesecloth. Let dry.

6 Trace wing onto dried, stiffened cheesecloth, using fabric pen. Lines of wing pattern should show through cheesecloth. Cut out. Glue curly hair to head as desired. Let dry.

7 If desired, paint entire angel and both sides of wings with gold spray paint, letting 1 side of wings dry before turning over. Apply glue to center of wings and position wings below head on back of angel. Use straight pins to hold wings in place until glue is dry. Drape wire-edged ribbon around back of angel and through arms (see photo). Tie ¼" ribbon in bow and glue below front of head. Let dry. For halo, glue ends of gold trim together. Let dry. Pin halo in place on top of head.

8 To store angel, wrap in tissue paper. Before using again, spritz with water and reshape.

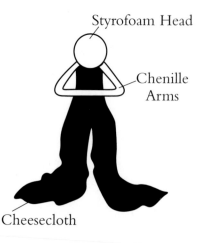

Styrofoam Head

Chenille Arms

Cheesecloth

Diagram

Design by Hancock Fabrics

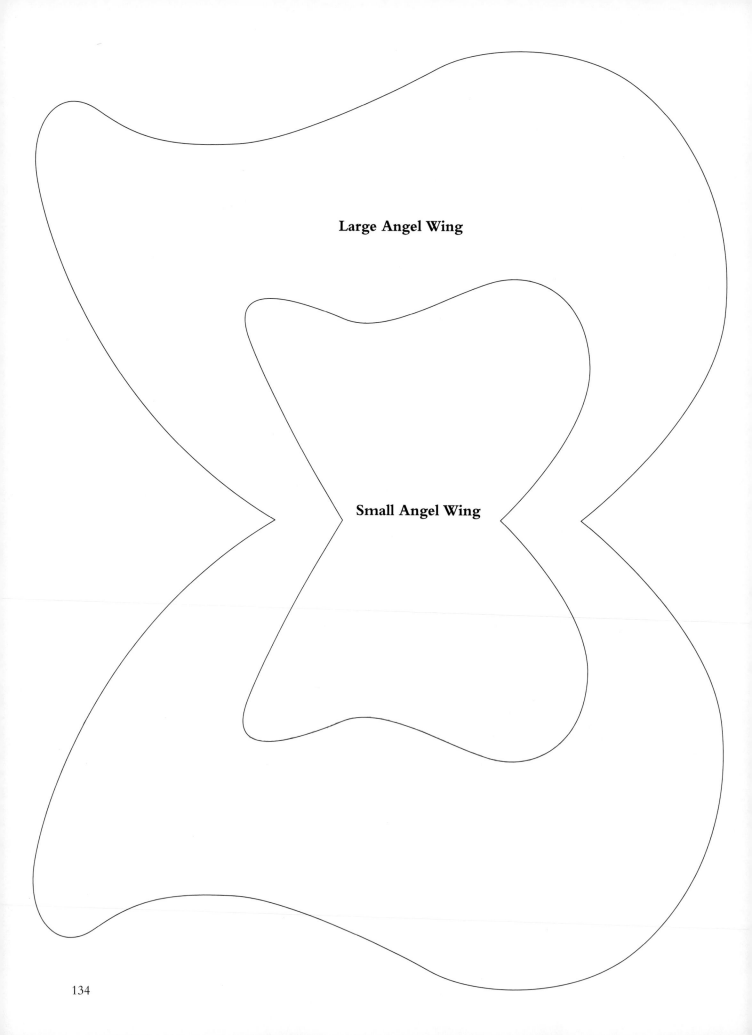

Large Angel Wing

Small Angel Wing

134

Reverse Foiled Ornaments

Make these bright balls in multiples for Christmas bazaars or ornament swaps.

Directions for 1 ornament

1 Separate ornament into 2 pieces. Tear pieces of tissue paper into 2" squares. Working on small area at a time, brush Reverse Collage Glue onto inside of each half of ornament. Press tissue paper squares onto glue-covered area. Brush another coat of glue over tissue paper. (Be sure to leave overlapping edges of ornament undecorated so that you can put ornament back together when dry.)

2 Punch out decorative shapes or circles from double-stick tape. Apply shapes to outside of ornament as desired. To apply gold foil, lay foil dull side down on top of tape shapes. Using finger, press foil onto tape, completely covering tape with foil. Peel away foil paper.

3 Reassemble ornament. Thread cording through hanger at top of ornament and knot ends. Tie wire-edged ribbon in bow. Hot-glue bow to top of ornament.

Designs by Lauren Johnston

135

Design by Cheryl Ball, SCD

Kid's Hands Tree Banner

This festive banner will be a hands-down favorite with parents and grandparents.

Materials

Fabrics: 18" x 23" piece red ticking, 18" x 23" piece white muslin for backing, 4 or 5 different green calico prints, red calico or plaid fabric
Aleene's Fusible Web™
Lightweight cardboard
Pinking shears
Aleene's Thick Designer Tacky Glue™
1 yard red metallic cording or ⅛"-wide red satin ribbon
10 gold jingle bells
Assorted buttons
Red dimensional fabric paint
Thread
20" length ¼"-diameter dowel

Directions

Note: See page 5 for tips on working with fusible web.

1 Using ticking as guide, cut web slightly smaller. Center and fuse web on back of ticking. Fuse ticking to wrong side of muslin, aligning edges.

2 Trace child's hand onto cardboard and cut out. Transfer pattern to paper side of fusible web 3 times; flip pattern over and transfer 3 more. Roughly cut out hands. Fuse hands to wrong side of green fabrics and cut out along marked lines.

3 Referring to photo for positioning, fuse cutouts to banner. Cut 1" x ½" strip of red fabric, using pinking shears; notch ends of strips, using regular scissors. Tie in bow and glue to top of hand tree. Let dry.

4 Trim banner, using pinking shears and leaving 1½" on each side of tree at widest point. Curve bottom of banner, leaving space for lettering (see photo). Cut straight across top of banner, 3" above top of tree.

5 Cut and tie cording or ribbon in 5 small bows. Glue bows, jingle bells, and buttons onto tree (see photo). Let dry. Using dimensional paint, paint wavy line around edge of banner; then write "Merry Christmas" or personalized message at bottom. Let dry.

6 For hanger, cut 3 (1½" x 45") strips from red fabric. Braid strips together, securing 3" from each end, using thread. Fold and glue top edge of banner over dowel. Let dry. Glue ends of braided section to ends of dowel (see photo). Let dry. Notch free ends of braided section. Glue buttons to cover thread-wrapped ends. Let dry.

Festive Fashion

Turn a plain purchased vest into a vest-ive garment for holiday parties, shopping, or work.

Materials

Denim vest
Desired fabric with tree motifs
Dark green felt
Aleene's Fusible Web™
Embroidery floss: gold, green scraps
Needle
Aleene's Premium-Coat™ Acrylic Paint: Yellow Ochre
Aleene's Enhancers™: Satin Varnish
Paintbrushes: #3 round, #10 flat
3 wooden star buttons
3 button covers
Aleene's Thick Designer Tacky Glue™

Directions

Note: See page 5 for tips on working with fusible web.

1 Wash and dry vest and fabric; do not use fabric softener in washer or dryer. If you wash felt, let it air-dry.

2 Using star patterns for Patriotic Felt Flag on page 114, transfer star patterns to paper side of fusible web. Or, if desired, draw stars freehand. Roughly cut out stars from fusible web. Fuse stars to felt and cut out along marked lines.

3 Blanket-stitch around neck and bottom of vest, using gold floss (see photo and Blanket-stitch Diagram). Cut desired tree motifs from fabric to fit inside stars (see photo). Fringe fabric edges. Then cut fabric to fit 1 corner of vest (see photo). Turn edges of corner piece under ¼". Cut web to fit corner piece and each motif. Fuse web pieces to wrong side of corresponding fabric pieces. Then fuse corner piece in place and 1 motif to each star. Fuse stars to vest where desired and then blanket stitch around stars, using gold floss.

4 Paint star buttons Yellow Ochre. Let dry. Apply 1 coat of varnish to each. Let dry. Tie 1 green floss scrap through holes in each button. Glue 1 star button to each button cover. Let dry.

5 Do not wash garment for at least 1 week. Turn garment wrong side out, wash by hand, and hang to dry.

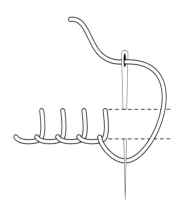

Blanket-stitch Diagram

Design by
Chris Wallace

Ginger
Garl

Design by Inga Johns

bread
and

Paper hearts and gingerbread
men dance along the bottom
of this colorful garland.

Materials

Brown paper bags

Aleene's Enhancers™: All-Purpose Primer, Satin Varnish

Aleene's Premium-Coat™ Acrylic Paints: White, True Red, True Green, Black

Paintbrushes: sponge, ½" flat shader, #2 liner, large glaze

Waxed paper

Paper towels

Wooden cutouts: 2 stocking ornaments, extra small hearts (1 for each gingerbread man)

Masking tape in various widths

Aleene's Tacky Glue™

2 large and 4 small jingle bells

Aleene's Satin Sheen Twisted Ribbon™: red

Artificial pine garland

26-gauge wire

Wire cutters

4 miniature grapevine wreaths

Cinnamon sticks

Pinecones

Red-and-green bead garland

Directions

1 For each design, transfer gingerbread man or heart pattern to brown paper and cut out. Using unthreaded sewing machine, stitch ¼" from edge to make perforated line (see photo on pages 140 and 141).

2 Brush all wooden and paper pieces with primer. Let dry. Apply 2 coats of White to heart and stocking ornaments, letting dry between coats and staying inside stitching line on hearts (see photo). Cut strips from various sizes of masking tape; place strips on hearts as desired, trimming to fit within stitching lines (see photo). Burnish edges of tape with fingernail so that paint won't seep under. Use shader brush to paint True Red between some strips and True Green between others. Let dry. Remove tape strips.

3 To paint highlights on heart ornaments, thin White with water. Load liner brush with thinned mixture and paint 1 line that follows curve at top of heart and another at opposite side near bottom (see photo). Let dry. Glue small jingle bell to top of each heart. Let dry.

4 To paint each gingerbread man, load liner brush with thinned White. Paint wavy lines for hair and edges of clothing; paint mouth and nose (see photo). Paint Black dots for eyes, using end of brush. Let dry. Wipe end of brush clean before dipping in next color. For each cheek, dip end of brush into True Red.

Paint 2 dots close to each other and then pull paint down from both dots to form heart. Let dry. Paint small dot in corner of each eye for highlights and dots down front of shape for buttons, using White. Let dry. Paint wooden hearts True Red. Let dry. Glue 1 to each gingerbread man (see photo). Let dry.

5 Apply 1 coat of varnish to all paper and wooden pieces. Let dry. Untwist 6' length of twisted ribbon. Using shader brush, paint White diagonal stripes along ribbon. Let dry. Paint True Green line on every other white stripe, using liner brush. Let dry. Apply 1 coat of varnish to painted areas. Let dry. Make small bows from painted twisted ribbon; attach to pine garland as desired (see photo).

6 To assemble, use wire to attach hearts and gingerbread men to pine garland as desired (see photo). Make 2 large bows, using remaining painted twisted ribbon and leaving 6" tails on each. Glue or wire 1 bow to each end of garland. Let dry. Glue 1 large jingle bell to center of each bow. Let dry. Wire candy cane stockings, grapevine wreaths, cinnamon sticks, pinecones, and bead garland to pine garland as desired.

Heart
Paint inside inner line.

Gingerbread Man

Christmas Tree Shirt

Outfit your family for the holidays in no-sew sweatshirts like this one.

Materials
½ yard green fabric
Crochet thread: green, red scrap, white
Large-eyed needle
Red sweatshirt
Aleene's Fusible Web™
Aleene's OK To Wash-It™ Glue
Buttons: 1 white star, assorted
Aleene's Jewel-It™ Glue

Directions

Note: See page 5 for tips on working with fusible web.

1 For tree branches, cut 4 (2" x 3") strips, 4 (2" x 5") strips, 4 (2" x 7") strips, and 4 (2" x 9") strips from fabric. Stack corresponding strips and join layers by making large stitches down middle of layered strips, using green crochet thread. Make small cuts through all layers of each stack, cutting almost to stitching line (see photo). Wet strips and place in dryer to fluff.

2 Wash and dry sweatshirt and remaining fabric; do not use fabric softener in washer or dryer.

3 For trunk, cut 1 (1" x 14") strip each from green fabric and web. Center and fuse trunk on sweatshirt. Referring to photo, position branches along trunk. Glue branches in place, using OK To Wash-It Glue. Let dry.

4 Tie red crochet thread scrap through holes in star button and white crochet thread through holes in remaining buttons. Glue star button to top of tree and remaining buttons onto tree branches, using Jewel-It Glue. To attach each button, squeeze puddle of glue in desired position. Press button into glue so that glue comes up through holes in button. Let dry.

5 Do not wash garment for at least 1 week. Turn garment wrong side out, wash by hand, and hang to dry.

Design by Penny Mathews

Index